"Anacker offers a careful and comprehensive guide to how deeply housing affects American social and economic life. Importantly, she also shows how to create inclusive, equitable and sustainable housing markets through local, state, and federal policy."

–**Dr Deirdre Pfeiffer,** Associate Professor,
School of Geographical Sciences and Urban Planning,
College of Liberal Arts and Sciences at Arizona State
University

"Housing is the biggest expense for most Americans and impacts many facets of public and private life. This book is an essential text that focuses on both of these aspects—housing's role as an economic engine, and the balkanized attempts of various levels of government to promote equity and efficiency in the provision of housing. Tackling each of these subjects is a major contribution by Anacker."

–**Dr Michael Lens**, Associate Professor of Urban
Planning and Public Policy at UCLA Luskin School
of Public Affairs

"This book offers a concise review of the key issues involved in housing markets and housing policy in the United States. Katrin Anacker is an expert guide who skillfully introduces and explains these important topics. The book will be an invaluable resource for students, instructors, and other readers."

–**Dr Shomon Shamsuddin**, Associate Professor,
Urban & Environment Policy & Planning at Tufts
University

T0372853

HOUSING IN THE UNITED STATES

Housing matters to people, be they owner, renter, housing provider, homeless individual, housing professional, or policymaker. *Housing in the United States: The Basics* offers an accessible introduction to key concepts and issues in housing—and a concise overview of the programs that affect housing choices, affordability, and access in the United States today. Part I covers the fundamentals of housing: households, housing units, and neighborhoods; housing as basic need vs. human right; supply and demand; construction, rehabilitation, and renovation; and demographic, socioeconomic, and cultural trends. Part II focuses on housing policy and its evolution from the early 20th century, through the Great Recession to the present day; policies related to owner- and renter-occupied housing; tax policies and expenditures; place- and people-based programs; and shortages of affordable housing.

Written in a clear and engaging style, this guide allows readers to quickly grasp the complex range of policies, programs, and factors that shape the housing landscape. Essential reading for students, community advocates, homebuyers/renters, and professionals with an interest in housing, it also serves as an ideal text for introductory courses in urban planning, urban studies, sociology, public administration, architecture, and real estate.

This book provides a valuable and practical foundation for informed housing discussions at the kitchen table, in the classroom, at work, or on Capitol Hill.

Katrin B. Anacker is currently a Professor at the Schar School of Policy and Government at George Mason University, VA, USA.

THE BASICS SERIES

The Basics is a highly successful series of accessible guidebooks which provide an overview of the fundamental principles of a subject area in a jargon-free and undaunting format.

Intended for students approaching a subject for the first time, the books both introduce the essentials of a subject and provide an ideal springboard for further study. With over 50 titles spanning subjects from artificial intelligence (AI) to women's studies, *The Basics* are an ideal starting point for students seeking to understand a subject area.

Each text comes with recommendations for further study and gradually introduces the complexities and nuances within a subject.

ELT
Michael McCarthy and Steve Walsh

SOLUTION-FOCUSED THERAPY
Yvonne Dolan

ACTING (THIRD EDITION)
Bella Merlin

BUSINESS ANTHROPOLOGY
Timothy de Waal Malefyt

EATING DISORDERS
Elizabeth McNaught, Janet Treasure, and Jess Griffiths

TRUTH
Jc Beall and Ben Middleton

PERCEPTION
Bence Nanay

C.G. JUNG'S COLLECTED WORKS
Ann Yeoman and Kevin Lu

CORPORATE FINANCE
Terence C.M. Tse

FILM GENRE
Barry Keith Grant

RELIGIONS AND SPORTS
Terry D. Shoemaker

CRITICAL THEORY
Martin Shuster

For a full list of titles in this series, please visit www.routledge.com/The-Basics/book-series/B

HOUSING IN THE UNITED STATES

STATES

THE BASICS

Katrin B. Anacker

Routledge
Taylor & Francis Group

NEW YORK AND LONDON

Designed cover image: © Shutterstock

First published 2024
by Routledge
605 Third Avenue, New York, NY 10158

and by Routledge
4 Park Square, Milton Park, Abingdon, Oxon, OX14 4RN

Routledge is an imprint of the Taylor & Francis Group, an informa business

© 2024 Katrin B. Anacker

Library of Congress Cataloging-in-Publication Data
Names: Anacker, Katrin B., author.
Title: Housing in the United States : the basics / Katrin B. Anacker.
Description: New York, NY: Routledge, 2024. |
Series: The basics | Includes bibliographical references and index.
Identifiers: LCCN 2023048723 (print) | LCCN 2023048724 (ebook) |
ISBN 9781032657639 (hardback) | ISBN 9781032655710 (paperback) |
ISBN 9781032657646 (ebook)
Subjects: LCSH: Housing—United States. | Housing policy—United States.
Classification: LCC HD7293 .A6888 2024 (print) | LCC HD7293 (ebook) |
DDC 363.50973—dc23/eng/20231026
LC record available at https://lccn.loc.gov/2023048723
LC ebook record available at https://lccn.loc.gov/2023048724

ISBN: 978-1-032-65763-9 (hbk)
ISBN: 978-1-032-65571-0 (pbk)
ISBN: 978-1-032-65764-6 (ebk)

DOI: 10.1201/9781032657646

Typeset in Bembo
by codeMantra

Für Mama und Papa
(nein, ihr braucht auch dieses Buch nicht zu lesen).

CONTENTS

PREFACE

WHAT IS THE BOOK ABOUT?

Housing in the United States: The Basics provides an overview of the U.S. housing market and housing policy. It discusses aspects of housing supply and demand impacting owner- and renter-occupied housing, as well as the programs, players, and processes that have shaped the U.S. housing landscape since the early 20th century.

Housing is important because it may contribute to a high quality of life at the individual and household levels, and it greatly contributes to the economy, although results about municipal costs and revenues are mixed. Expenditures for housing are typically one of the largest parts of a household's monthly budget. For some homeowners, homeownership may be a stable and often largest foundation for achieving long-term wealth due to continued property value appreciation. For some renters, a home may be a temporary place, characterized by a maintenance-free lifestyle, as the vast majority of repairs and routine maintenance are deferred to a housing provider.

Stakeholders in housing may be residents, regardless of whether they live in owner- or renter-occupied housing units, local, regional, state, and national governments, as well as the housing industry, for example, developers, builders, realtors, appraisers, insurers, home inspectors, housing providers, mortgage and insurance specialists, architects, and urban planners, among many others.

Public policy, or a system of guidelines, laws, and programs issued by federal, state, and local governments, responds to societal challenges and needs, as well as market failures. Housing policy focuses on homelessness and affordable housing, including homeownership, among many other aspects.

WHO IS THIS BOOK FOR?

Housing in the United States: The Basics may be of interest to students in the social sciences, including urban planning, urban geography, urban sociology, and urban policy. It may also be of interest to people excited about current events.

HOW IS THIS BOOK ORGANIZED?

This book is organized in two parts. Part I discusses housing in general, including the importance of housing, the connection between housing and neighborhoods, housing as a basic need versus housing as a right, the impacts on housing supply, the impacts on housing demand, and housing affordability. Part II discusses housing policy, focusing on the importance of housing policy, owner-occupied housing, and renter-occupied housing.

ACKNOWLEDGMENTS

Over the past few years, many colleagues have supported this project. Editor Lisa Mosier, Editorial Assistant Kirsty Hardwick, and other members on the team were a pleasure to work with. Bernadette Hanlon kindly suggested submitting the manuscript to *The Basics* series when I was looking for a publisher home. Rebecca Walter and Kirk McClure provided helpful suggestions on the first draft and five anonymous reviewers gave constructive comments on the second draft. In particular, Reviewers D and E provided detailed line-by-line comments on the second draft (thank you!) and Reviewer E even provided additional comments and suggestions on the third draft (thank you so much!). My invaluable and patient personal copy editor Matt Ogborn improved several drafts. Rajendra Kulkarni fine-tuned several figures on a rather short notice. All of my colleagues' contributions improved the manuscript, and all errors and mistakes are mine.

Kingsley Haynes and Jim Finkelstein hired me during the Great Recession, when I needed a new academic home on a very short notice. I cannot imagine where I would now be without that sponsor letter, work visa, and letter of offer! Arlington County's Department of Parks and Recreation provides an award-winning, wonderful, interconnected trail system, including the lovely Bluemont Junction Trail, the delightful Four Mile Run Trail, and the efficient W&OD Trail ("passing on your left!"), enabling me to hash things out during rejuvenating late afternoon runs. Thank you! Lastly, I dedicate this book to my parents, Jürgen and Erika Anacker, who have been supporting me in innumerable ways over many, many years. *Und wie immer – nein, ihr braucht auch dieses Buch nicht zu lesen.*

ABBREVIATIONS

ACS	American Community Survey
AFCI	arc-fault circuit interrupter
AGI	adjusted gross income
AMGI	Area Median Gross Income
AMI	area median income
ARRA	American Recovery and Reinvestment Act
B&L	building and loan (societies)
BMIR	Below Market Interest Rate
CARES Act	Coronavirus Aid, Relief, and Economic Security Act
CCP	Consumer Credit Panel
CDBG	Community Development Block Grant
CDC	Centers for Disease Control and Prevention
CDC	Community Development Corporation
CFPB	Consumer Financial Protection Bureau
CHA	Chicago Housing Authority
COVID	corona virus disease
CRA	Community Reinvestment Act
DIY	do-it-yourself
ECOA	Equal Credit Opportunity Act
EESA	Emergency Economic Stabilization Act
EHFP	Equitable Housing Finance Plan
EO	Executive Order
EPA	(U.S.) Environmental Protection Agency
ERA	Emergency Rental Assistance
FCRA	Federal Credit Reform Act
FDIC	Federal Deposit Insurance Corporation
FFIEC	Federal Financial Institutions Examination Council

FHA	Federal Housing Administration
FHFA	Federal Housing Finance Agency
FHFB	Federal Housing Finance Board
FHLB	Federal Home Loan Bank (system)
FHLMC	Federal Home Loan Mortgage Corporation (Freddie Mac)
FICO®	Fair Isaac Corporation
FMR	Fair Market Rent
FNMA	Federal National Mortgage Association (Fannie Mae)
FOMC	Federal Open Market Committee
FRED	Federal Reserve Economic Data
GDP	Gross domestic product
GFCI	ground-fault circuit interrupter
GNMA	Government National Mortgage Association (Ginnie Mae)
GSEs	government-sponsored enterprises
H4H	Hope for Homeowners
HAMP	Home Affordable Mortgage Program
HARP	Home Affordable Refinance Program
HCAI	Housing Credit Availability Index
HCV	Housing Choice Voucher
HERA	Housing and Economic Recovery Act
HFA	housing finance agency
HMDA	Home Mortgage Disclosure Act
HMI	Housing Market Index
HOEPA	Home Ownership and Equity Protection Act
HOLC	Home Owners' Loan Corporation
HOPE	Homeownership Opportunities for People Everywhere
HUD	(U.S.) Department of Housing and Urban Development
IMB	independent mortgage bank
IRS	Internal Revenue Service
LIHTC	Low Income Housing Tax Credit
LTV	loan-to-value
MBS	mortgage-backed security
MHA	Making Home Affordable
MID	Mortgage Interest Deduction

MIP	mortgage insurance premium
MMI	Mutual Mortgage Insurance (Fund)
MSA	Metropolitan Statistical Area
MTO	Moving to Opportunity
NAACP	National Association for the Advancement of Colored People
NAHB	National Association of Home Builders
NBER	National Bureau of Economic Research
NC/SR	New Construction and Substantial Rehabilitation
NFMC	National Foreclosure Mitigation Counseling
NIMBY	not in my backyard
NLIHC	National Low Income Housing Coalition
NSPs	Neighborhood Stabilization Programs
OECD	Organisation for Economic Co-operation and Development
PDMDA	Presidentially Declared Major Disaster Area
PHA	public housing authorities/agency
PMI	private mortgage insurance
PPP	Paycheck Protection Program
PRIZM	Potential Rating Index for Zipcode Markets
PWA	Public Works Administration
QAP	Qualified Allocation Plan
QCT	Qualified Census Tract
RAD	Rental Assistance Demonstration
REO	Real Estate Owned
RESPA	Real Estate Settlement Procedures Act
RFC	Reconstruction Finance Corporation
S&L	savings and loan (societies)
SNAP	Supplemental Nutrition Assistance Program
SPCP	Special Purpose Credit Program
SR	Special Rapporteur
TARP	Troubled Asset Relief Program
TCJA	Tax Cut and Jobs Act
TIF	tax increment financing
TILA	Truth in Lending Act
UN	United Nations
USDA	U.S. Department of Agriculture
VA	(U.S.) Department of Veterans Affairs
WIC	Women, Infants, and Children

PART I

HOUSING IN THE UNITED STATES

This Part provides an overview of the U.S. housing market and housing policy. It discusses aspects of housing supply and demand, impacting owner- and renter-occupied housing. Housing and neighborhoods mean many things to many people. Households, housing units, and neighborhoods undergo change over time. Regional and local stakeholders may influence neighborhoods. Abraham Maslow's hierarchy of human needs encompasses five consecutive levels of need: two physical needs (physiological needs and security and safety needs) and three social needs (sense of belonging, self-esteem or ego needs, and self-actualization needs). Although there is no right to housing in the U.S., it is an aspirational ideal embedded in Article 25 of the Universal Declaration of Human Rights of the United Nations.

Housing supply and building cycles are influenced by many factors, including the state of the economy, access to mortgages and mortgage interest rates, developer market assessments, zoning, community response, housing policy, and housing demand. Housing demand is influenced by many factors, including the population, household sizes, household incomes, family lifecycle stages, generational groups, and housing policy. Housing affordability is a policy concern, as households burdened with high housing expenditures may have fewer resources left to pay for food, utilities, health and child care expenditures, transportation to work, emergencies, retirement, and professional opportunities, such as pursuing higher education or starting a business.

DOI: 10.1201/9781032657646-1

INTRODUCTION
The Importance of Housing

Housing is important because it may contribute to a high quality of life at the individual and household levels, and it contributes a great amount to the economy, although results about municipal costs and revenues are mixed. Housing is important at several levels. At the *individual* and *household* level, a home may be a *permanent* place, characterized by household, housing, and neighborhood stability that result in a high quality of life (Kusenbach & Paulsen, 2013; Sherman, 2017). Purchasing a home is often the biggest investment an individual or a household makes (Weinstock, 2023). Expenditures for housing (i.e., mortgage payments, rent, expenditures for utility services, maintenance, or repairs) are typically one of the largest parts of a household's monthly budget (Bull & Gross, 2023; Iglesias, 2009; Stone, 2006). For some homeowners, homeownership may be a *stable* and often the *largest* foundation for achieving long-term wealth due to continued property value appreciation (McCabe, 2016). For others, including homeowners of manufactured units who own their homes but typically lease the land on which their units are sitting, homeownership may mean eviction when the housing provider does not renew a lease, or foreclosure when a borrower can no longer afford to make monthly payments (Sullivan, 2018). An evicted homeowner may then bounce from one couch to another, live in a car, or even live on the street, ultimately having difficulties recovering their life (Salamon & MacTavish, 2017).

For some renters, a home may be a *temporary* place, characterized by household, housing, and neighborhood challenges that result in a low

DOI: 10.1201/9781032657646-2

quality of life (Botein & Hetling, 2016; Desmond, 2016; Freeman, 2019). For others, it may be a place characterized by a maintenance-free lifestyle, as the vast majority of repairs and routine maintenance are deferred to a housing provider (Stueve et al., 2018). For many others, renting may translate into flexibility to move, incurring relatively small costs within a relatively short time frame (Stueve et al., 2018). Renting may mean relatively predictable monthly costs, at least until the end of the current month, if not the end of the lease (Stueve et al., 2018). For other renters, renting may cause uncertainty because rents may increase, making units unaffordable, or because housing providers may terminate leases (Shaw, 2018).

At the *national* level, the entire U.S. housing stock was worth $45.3 trillion in December 2022, equaling about 178% of the nation's gross domestic product (GDP), which is the national total value of goods produced and services provided during one year ($25.46 trillion; Bureau of Economic Analysis, 2023; Katz & Zhao, 2023). In 2021, all spending on housing services (i.e., spending on rents and imputed rents or a homeowner's hypothetical willingness to pay to live in one's home) and utilities was about $2.8 trillion, translating into 11.9% of the GDP (Weinstock, 2023). In 2021, all spending on residential fixed investment (i.e., spending on new construction, rehabilitation, remodeling, and brokers' fees) was about $1.1 trillion, which is the equivalent of 4.8% of the GDP (Weinstock, 2023). Thus, total spending on housing constituted 16.7% of the GDP, or nearly as much as total spending on healthcare (18.3% of the GDP), making housing and healthcare the two largest components of the GDP (Centers for Medicare and Medicaid Services, n.d.; Weinstock, 2023).

In terms of economic impact, and focusing on revenues, building an *average single-family home* (construction value: $421,000; sale price: $498,060) generated 2.90 full-time jobs and $129,647 in taxes in 2020 (Emrath, 2020; the most recent information as of this writing). Building an *average rental apartment* (construction value: $169,000) generated 1.25 full-time jobs and $55,909 in taxes, and $100,000 spent on remodeling generated 0.75 full-time jobs and $29,797 in taxes, based on all state and local governments in the U.S. (more than 89,000; Emrath, 2020; the most recent information as of this writing). These jobs generated are in industries that create products, including lumber, concrete, or heating equipment, or that provide services, including transporting, storing, or selling these products for constructing, rehabilitating, and renovating homes (Emrath, 2020). Examples of taxes used for revenue at the *federal* level are income taxes (paid by corporations, receivers of dividends from corporations, proprietors, and employees), government social insurance (paid by employers), and excise taxes and customs duties (Emrath, 2020). Examples of taxes used for revenue at the *state and local* level are income taxes, permits, hook-ups, impacts, other fees, sales taxes, and other business taxes and license fees (Emrath, 2020).

Focusing on *revenues* compared to *costs and capital investments*, building 100 new, average single-family homes and 100 new, average rental apartments in 2015 generated $10.6 million in taxes and other revenues for state and local governments, compared to $4.2 million in expenditures ($1 million) and capital investments ($3.2 million) for public services by all state and local governments in the U.S. (more than 89,000; National Association of Home Builders, 2015a, 2015b; the most recent information as of this writing). After the *first year*, these 100 new, average single-family homes and rental apartments generated $2.4 million in taxes and other revenues, compared to $2.1 million in expenditures for public services by state and local governments (National Association of Home Builders, 2015a, 2015b). After *15 years*, these buildings were predicted to generate $44.4 million in revenues and $33.5 million in expenditures (National Association of Home Builders, 2015a, 2015b). Alternatively, the American Farmland Trust found that one dollar of municipal revenue raised leads to $1.16 of median costs for municipal services for residential developments, based on an analysis of 151 communities in the U.S. (American Farmland Trust, 2016; the most recent information as of this writing).

2

HOUSING IN NEIGHBORHOODS

Homes are typically clustered in *neighborhoods*, which mean many things to many people. Some neighborhoods may have well-constructed and well-maintained housing stocks, high-income households, and high-quality public and private infrastructure and amenities, such as roads, bridges, water and sewerage pipes, street lights, telecommunications and internet, broadband, schools, and so-called *third places*, a term coined by Oldenburg (1999). Examples of third places are restaurants, cafés, and bars, among others (Kusenbach & Paulsen, 2013). These factors may result in high property values, rapid property value appreciation, high community pride, tightly-knit community bonds, and thus an overall high quality of life (Galster, 2019). Other neighborhoods may have challenged housing stocks, low-income households, and low-quality public and private infrastructure and amenities, resulting in low property values and slow or no property value appreciation, vacancies, vandalism, crime, and thus an overall low quality of life (Betancur & Smith, 2016). Some neighborhoods may be *more dense*, for example, in inner cities, while others may be *less dense*, for example, in outer suburbs or rural areas (Anacker, 2015c). While many may label these neighborhoods as "hell," others may consider them a "haven" (Freeman, 2019).

Most households, housing units, and neighborhoods undergo change over time. *Household demographic change* happens when the composition of households changes over the life course, such as when children are born or adopted, adult children leave the home to attend college, adult children return home after college, adults (re-)

DOI: 10.1201/9781032657646-3

establish or combine households, seniors move in with their adult children and vice versa, or when residents die (Burns & Porter, 2016; Sassler & Miller, 2017). *Household economic change* occurs when there are changes in the number of earners and changes in household income due to earnings, either through formal or informal work, capital investments, or renting out space in the home, which is facilitated by recently established home-sharing platforms such as Airbnb, among others (Benson, 2007; Morduch & Schneider, 2017).

Housing unit change happens when homeowners or housing providers build or modify structures, including when they construct an entirely new building; renovate, rehabilitate, or demolish an existing building; or add to or raze parts of an existing building (Aktas & Bilec, 2012). Housing unit change also occurs when one or several units are combined or divided into a multifamily building to accommodate a growing household or a growing number of households (Brown, 2015). Housing unit change may also occur when a building inspector in the respective local government discovers that building codes have been violated, mandating that a homeowner or housing provider make changes to bring the building up to code (Bartram, 2022; Desmond, 2016).

Neighborhood change occurs when housing units are added, modified (e.g., conversions from one-level Cape Cod homes to two-level modern farmhouses), or lost (i.e., because of natural disasters, fires, teardowns, or moved to other sites; Harris, 2012; Kaysen, 2023; Kirby & Hardison-Moody, 2018; Philp, 2017). It also occurs when there is investment (or lack thereof) in public and private infrastructure and amenities (Detter & Fölster, 2017).

Furthermore, neighborhood change occurs when there is residential succession (i.e., changes in the number of residents via in-movers and out-movers) and the housing stock (i.e., through capital improvements – or a lack thereof). Moreover, neighborhood change occurs when there are socioeconomic changes between in-movers and out-movers (i.e., gentrification or decline; Galster, 2019; Talen, 2019). These changes may possibly result in overcrowding, on the one hand, or vacancies, on the other (Econometrica et al., 2007). Overcrowding, including having more than one person per room in a housing unit, is undesirable because it may facilitate the spread of communicable diseases such as meningitis, hepatitis, and tuberculosis, negatively impact a child's growth and development, and strain household relationships (Econometrica et al., 2007). Householders may alleviate overcrowding by moving to larger units, but these may be difficult if not impossible to find in places with a shortage of affordable housing, which is discussed below.

Vacancies can come in many forms. The U.S. Bureau of the Census distinguishes among the following types of vacancies: "(a) vacant for rent; (b) rented, but not yet occupied; (c) vacant for sale; (d) sold, but not yet occupied; (e) maintained for seasonal, recreational, and occasional use; and (f) other vacant" (Mallach, 2018, p. 10). Whereas some vacancies may be tolerated, such as the first two types, as they provide slack in a healthy housing market, others are undesirable because they may negatively impact the quality of life in a neighborhood, the property values of adjacent properties, and local government budgets, affecting expenditures for policing, code enforcement and compliance, and possibly building demolition (Mallach, 2018). Neighborhoods with very high vacancy rates higher than 14% or even 20%, depending on the author, may be termed "hypervacant" (Harrison & Immergluck, 2021; Mallach, 2018). In some of these hypervacant neighborhoods, the number and proportion of vacant properties may increase rapidly and the housing market may no longer function (Mallach, 2018). Over the past few decades, the number of hypervacant neighborhoods, especially in the Rustbelt, has increased (Harrison & Immergluck, 2021). Potential solutions could be removing obstacles to reuse, such as spot blight eminent domain (i.e., when a municipality takes an individual abandoned parcel and sells it to a new owner); vacant property receivership (i.e., when a local court designates a new owner who receives an individual abandoned building); or land banking (i.e., when counties or municipalities hold, maintain, or transfer vacant properties; Mallach 2018). Other solutions could be building local markets, demolition, and green reuses through community gardens or vacant lot greenings (Mallach, 2018).

There are many *local and regional stakeholders* that deal with household, housing, and neighborhood change. For example, homeowners and housing providers may engage in capital improvement activities whenever they anticipate a positive return on their investment as a neighborhood is doing well (Allon, 2008). Homeowners and housing providers may also contact their respective local governments to assist them in looking for national, state, or local public programs to obtain funding, which in turn is administered by the local government (Kinder, 2016). Renters, who may decide to stay in or move to a neighborhood because it is affordable or amenable to them, may contact their local government to report housing unit and neighborhood challenges, such as a housing unit not being up to code or the neighborhood needing trash removal (Bartram, 2022).

Local governments are also stakeholders. They zone land, determining the use, type, and size of buildings; they provide building inspections to ensure that occupied as well as vacant buildings are safe to live and work in; and they provide property assessments to determine property taxes, which in turn fund local K-12 schools and the local and regional infrastructures, including police and fire stations, roads, bridges, parks, and police, fire, and municipal vehicles and personnel (Glaeser & Gyourko, 2018; Keefer, 2018; Rybczynski, 2007; Straus, 2014). Interestingly, both *fiscal authority* (i.e., raising taxes to fund spending, cutting non-essential government functions, and decreasing spending) and *vocal populism* (i.e., a political movement that juxtaposes the people against the elite) have been somewhat on the rise recently, resulting in power shifting from the *federal to the state* and from the *state to the local level*, while also shifting tasks from the *public* to the *private* or *nonprofit* sectors (Hayes, 2020; Mudde & Kaltwasser, 2017). Thus, local governments, private companies, nonprofit organizations, citizen groups, and even single citizens have funded or taken on tasks previously funded and undertaken by federal, state, and local governments (Adams, 2014; Fallows & Fallows, 2019). Some have called this movement the New Localism (Katz & Nowak, 2017), while others have discussed "do-it-yourself cities" or "help-yourself cities" (Douglas, 2018). For example, over the past decade or so, Detroit has evolved into a do-it-yourself city in which residents have engaged in many activities that were previously associated with the local government, such as watching or patrolling blocks, boarding up abandoned homes, sweeping streets, mowing lawns, and removing snow, among many other activities (Kinder, 2016). Do-it-yourself (DIY) urban design encompasses "unauthorized, yet intentionally functional and civic-minded improvements to urban spaces" that go beyond official streetscape planning and design elements, such as homemade signs and benches, guerrilla bike lanes, or little free libraries or pantries (Douglas, 2018, p. 3).

A final example of stakeholders is *local businesses, developers, builders, realtors, appraisers, title insurers, home inspectors, housing providers, mortgage and insurance specialists*, and *architects*, all of whom may be interested in analyzing household, housing, and neighborhood changes to assess risk and predict whether their investments will pay off (Bartram, 2022; Bruin & Mitchell, 2018). For example, businesses pay attention to demographic and socioeconomic factors to calculate disposable income and thus predict spending or rely on neighborhood categorization services provided by Claritas or PRIZM (Potential Rating Index for Zipcode Markets) (Committee on Small Business, 2019; Talen, 2019). Developers and builders construct or rehabilitate structures, realtors buy and sell homes, housing providers rent out homes, and mortgage and insurance businesses originate or refinance loans or insure properties, analyzing and predicting spatial factors that may influence their investments (Kirsch & Squires, 2017; Rascoff & Humphries, 2015). While some stakeholders may view housing as an investment, as discussed above, others may see it as a basic need, and still others may see it as a right, as discussed in Chapter 3.

HOUSING AS A BASIC NEED VERSUS HOUSING AS A RIGHT

3.1 HOUSING AS A BASIC NEED

The minimum, bottom, or "floor" perspective regards housing as a basic need, as exemplified by Abraham Maslow's hierarchy of human needs, first published in 1942 (Hays, 2012; Maslow, 1970). Within the basic need for housing, there are human physical versus human social needs.

Maslow's Human Physical Needs

Maslow's hierarchy encompasses five consecutive levels of need that the vast majority of humans try to satisfy. The first of the two physical needs is *physiological needs*, including food, protection from the elements, and the ability to maintain one's body temperature (Beamish & Goss, 2018). Physiological needs may not be fulfilled if a person is homeless and sleeping in public shelters or places not meant for habitation, such as streets (Colburn & Aldern, 2022). Homelessness may be caused by broad economic factors, structural factors, personal factors, or the complex interaction among them (Colburn & Aldern, 2022). Broad economic factors may be an economic recession that causes unemployment or a constrained local housing market, which could result in high and thus unaffordable rents and a low number of vacancies (Colburn & Aldern, 2022). Structural factors may be racial, ethnic, gender, age, or sexual preference discrimination (Colburn & Aldern, 2022). Personal factors may be prior public shelter use,

DOI: 10.1201/9781032657646-4

residential instability, lack or dearth of social capital, veteran status, and mental illness and substance abuse (Willse, 2015).

One strategy to end homelessness is financial housing assistance, which may include assistance with rent, security deposits, move-in costs, or utility payments, in addition to referrals to social services, such as Medicaid and cash assistance (Colburn & Aldern, 2022). Another strategy is transitional housing to address social service needs and stabilize clients before they move into permanent (supportive) housing (Colburn & Aldern, 2022). Until about two decades ago, most clients had to demonstrate sobriety from drugs or alcohol, show improvement in mental health status, or participate in social services before they were allowed into permanent (supportive) housing (Colburn & Aldern, 2022). However, Housing First has been a somewhat recent approach to prevent or decrease homelessness by rapidly rehousing people through short-term and highly flexible assistance while not requiring sobriety, improved mental health, or service enrollment (Willse, 2015). Having a place to live means individuals are better able to address substance abuse challenges; pursue education, training, or find a job; and possibly not need outpatient or inpatient hospital utilization, thus reducing criminal justice involvement and public services use (National Alliance to End Homelessness, 2016).

Physiological needs are also unfulfilled if a person is not protected from the elements due to flooding that affects area homes or rain that hits leaky roofs or windows. Flooding may affect residents who live in a flood zone or in an area struck by disasters such as tornados, hurricanes, cyclones, or excessive rainfall (Kirby & Hardison-Moody, 2018). Leaky roofs or windows may be caused by a lack of maintenance over time (Kirby & Hardison-Moody, 2018). Strategies to address these physiological needs are avoiding building in or moving out of a flood zone; preparing well for disaster by, for example, covering windows and exterior doors; having regular home inspections that include the roof, windows, and heating and cooling equipment; and maintaining and investing in the home (Kirby & Hardison-Moody, 2018).

The second of the physical needs is *security and safety needs*. *External* home security and safety needs may be met by living in a unit that has a front door with a functioning lock and possibly an alarm system. *Internal* home security and safety needs may be satisfied by the lack or dearth of home fires, common home hazards, and toxins, as discussed below. Home fires, which may cause death, may be triggered by preparing food on a stove or in an oven, operating heating equipment, operating electrical equipment, smoking, or burning candles (Flanders, 2014; National Fire Protection Association, n.d.).

Strategies for preventing home fires are being present while a stove or oven is on, while heating equipment is running, during smoking, and while candles are burning, as well as using a timer (National Fire Protection Association, n.d.). Other strategies are turning off any heating equipment before going to bed, keeping anything flammable at least 3 feet from cooking or heating equipment, considering quitting smoking, only smoking outside, keeping anything flammable a safe distance from ashtrays, using deep and sturdy ashtrays, and dousing cigarette butts in water or sand (Flanders, 2014; National Fire Protection Association, n.d.). Other strategies are to use arc-fault circuit interrupters (AFCIs) and ground-fault circuit interrupters (GFCIs) that shut off electricity when a dangerous situation occurs, have major appliances directly plugged into an outlet (i.e., not use extension cords or plug strips), regularly check and test electrical cords, unplug electrical equipment while it is not in use, have only one electrical device plugged in and running at a time, and use the right number of watts for light bulbs (National Fire Protection Association, n.d.).

Furthermore, residents can establish "no-go" zones for children of at least 3 feet around stoves, ovens, and heating equipment; install child-proof devices for outlets; and keep smoking materials out of the reach of children (National Fire Protection Association, n.d.). Finally, other strategies include having a professional inspect a new home or regularly inspect an existing home, especially after a rehabilitation or renovation, having a professional install any heating or electrical equipment, and regularly testing fire alarms (National Fire Protection Association, n.d.).

In addition to home hazards that may cause home fires, other internal home security and safety needs may be a lack or dearth of common home hazards that can cause seniors to fall, possibly resulting in complicated hip fractures and even fatal head injuries (Centers for Disease Control and Prevention, n.d.a; Torres, 2019). Falls may also occur due to home-related factors such as broken or uneven steps, throw rugs or clutter that can be tripped over, long runs of stairs, or bathrooms and hallways that lack grab bars (Hartje et al., 2018; Parrott & Beamish, 2018). Some falls may occur outside of the home due to increased activities of seniors (Torres, 2019). Many falls occur due to personal factors, such as lower body weakness, difficulties with walking and balance, use of medicines that may affect balance, vision problems, poor footwear, or the refusal to use a walking aid (Centers for Disease Control and Prevention, n.d.a; Torres, 2019). Falls may also occur because there is little awareness of fall prevention, which could be achieved through balance training.

In addition to home hazards that may cause home fires or that can cause seniors to fall, as discussed above, other home hazards are toxins such as asbestos, combustion gases, lead, mold, and radon, all of which may trigger allergic reactions, asthma, other respiratory complaints, and poisoning in the short run and possibly chronic diseases or cancer in the long run (Allen & Macomber, 2020).

Asbestos

Asbestos, a mineral fiber with good strength and heat resistance that naturally occurs in rock and soil, was commonly used in building construction for insulation and as a fire retardant until 1980, when it was severely restricted for some uses and banned for others by the U.S. Environmental Protection Agency (EPA) (U.S. Environmental Protection Agency, n.d.a). However, it is still present in buildings constructed before it was restricted (Anacker et al., 2018). While asbestos–containing materials in good working condition typically do not pose health risks, damaged or disturbed materials do (U.S. Environmental Protection Agency, n.d.a). Asbestos fibers and particles become hazardous when they are released into the air due to material damage, home renovation, rehabilitation, or demolition (U.S. Environmental Protection Agency, n.d.a). Asbestos may be found in attic and wall insulations; vinyl floor tiles; the backing on vinyl sheet flooring and adhesives; roofing and siding shingles; textured paint and patching compounds in walls and ceilings; walls and floors around wood-burning stoves protected with asbestos paper, millboard, or cement sheets; hot water and steam pipes coated with asbestos material or covered with an asbestos blanket or tape; or oil furnaces and door gaskets with asbestos insulation (U.S. Environmental Protection Agency, n.d.a). Exposure to asbestos may ultimately cause lung cancer, mesothelioma (i.e., cancer that resides in the thin lining of the lung, chest, abdomen, and heart), and asbestosis, a disease of the lungs (U.S. Environmental Protection Agency, n.d.a). Strategies to deal with exposure to asbestos in a building are encapsulation, enclosure, or environmental remediation of the affected area by a trained and accredited professional (U.S. Environmental Protection Agency, n.d.a).

Combustion Gases

Combustion gases may be emitted by any aging or malfunctioning equipment that burns gas, oil, wood, coal, or kerosene, such as space heaters, water heaters, or equipment for cooking, furnaces, ranges/ ovens, or clothes dryers (Parrott & Atiles, 2018). Aging or malfunctioning equipment may result in combustion gases re-entering the home, causing back drafting or "spilling" into the home (Parrott & Atiles, 2018). Combustion gases may negatively impact indoor air quality and trigger high moisture, leading to mold, odors, and a high amount of airborne chemicals that can result in choking, suffocation, and even home fires (Parrott & Atiles, 2018).

Lead

Lead occurs naturally but may cause challenges when found in high concentrations in lead-based paint, lead-contaminated soils, and drinking water (U.S. Department of Housing and Urban Development, n.d.e; U.S. Environmental Protection Agency, n.d.b). Exposure to lead can cause damage to the nervous system, kidneys, and reproductive system (Parrott & Atiles, 2018). Lead-based paint was commonly used in home construction before 1940, and its use gradually decreased until 1978, when it was banned by the U.S. Environmental Protection Agency (U.S. Environmental Protection Agency, n.d.b). Many mature neighborhoods in inner cities and mature suburbs, both of which are home to a high proportion of people of color, are still impacted by lead-based paint (Frey, 2018a).

Lead-based paint that is present under layers of newer paint typically does not pose health risks (U.S. Environmental Protection Agency, n.d.b). However, paint that resides on surfaces that have much wear and tear, such as window frames and window sills, doors, door frames, stairs, railings, banisters, and porches, can peel, chip, chalk, crack, or be damaged (U.S. Environmental Protection Agency, n.d.b). Lead-based paint chips taste sweet and may be ingested by young children, and lead-based odors that are released through cracks may be inhaled by anyone (U.S. Environmental Protection Agency, n.d.b). In order to deal with lead-based paint, short-term strategies are frequent airing, dusting, and cleaning, while long-term strategies are demolishing or painting surfaces with lead-free paint (U.S. Environmental Protection Agency, n.d.b). Another strategy is moving to buildings built after 1978.

Lead-contaminated soils may be present at sites that formerly housed gas stations or industrial plants or on sites that currently house structures with exterior surfaces with deteriorating paint, where lead-contaminated flakes or peels are washed into the soil (U.S. Environmental Protection Agency, n.d.b). Lead in soil may be ingested by young children through hand-to-mouth activity or by anyone who eats fruit and vegetables produced on contaminated sites (U.S. Environmental Protection Agency, n.d.b). Lead in soil may also be inhaled by anyone who plays or works on a site (U.S. Environmental Protection Agency, n.d.b). In order to deal with lead-contaminated soils, short-term strategies may encompass taking off one's shoes at the front door, using door mats, and washing one's hands after playing or working outdoors (U.S. Environmental Protection Agency, n.d.b). Long-term strategies may be to plant bushes and trees (so children will not play on the soil), move to a different home, or complete environmental remediation (Riismandel, 2020; U.S. Environmental Protection Agency, n.d.b).

Lead in drinking water may be triggered by water service lines and household plumbing materials that have lead pipes and lead solders, brass well pumps, and brass fixtures, all of which were commonly used until 1986 (U.S. Environmental Protection Agency, n.d.b). Challenges may especially occur when plumbing materials are corroded, which may be triggered by water with high acidity or low mineral content (Highsmith, 2015; U.S. Environmental Protection Agency, n.d.b). Strategies to deal with lead in drinking water are to buy bottled water in the short run and to perform corrosion control treatment or to replace the infrastructure in the long run (Riismandel, 2020; U.S. Environmental Protection Agency, n.d.b).

Mold

Mold is a fungus that occurs naturally in outdoor and indoor environments and thus is impossible to completely eliminate (U.S. Environmental Protection Agency, n.d.c). Mold may grow on skin cells, residues from soap or shampoo, textiles, wallpaper, drywall, carpet, insulation materials, and wood, among other substances (Allen & Macomber, 2020). Mold may become an issue when there is humidity above 50%, excess moisture, water leaks, or flooding, but also when there is a lack of or insufficient level of proper ventilation (Parrott & Atiles, 2018). Short-term strategies to address mold are ventilating bathrooms, laundry/dryer rooms, and kitchens by opening windows and doors; using air conditioners, dehumidifiers, and exhaust fans; and heating indoor areas (U.S. Environmental Protection Agency, n.d.c). Mid-term strategies are cleaning and drying any damp or wet building materials and furnishings; installing a constantly running, low-volume fan that increases its capacity whenever the light is turned on in a bathroom; and addressing leakages and plumbing issues (U.S. Environmental Protection Agency, n.d.c). Long-term strategies are reducing the potential for condensation on cold surfaces by adding insulation; preventing or replacing moldy materials, including removing carpeting and installing (glazed) tiles or engineered stone in areas that have a perpetual moisture problem, such as near drinking fountains or sinks; and using products with antimicrobial finishes or additives, such as paints with fungicides (U.S. Environmental Protection Agency, n.d.c).

Radon

Radon occurs when radioactive uranium is naturally broken down in soil, rock, or water and then released into the air, where it is invisible, odorless, and tasteless (U.S. Environmental Protection Agency, n.d.d). Radon may enter the lining of the lungs, damage lung cells, and ultimately cause lung cancer, especially among smokers (Allen & Macomber, 2020; American Cancer Society, n.d.). Whereas radon levels cannot be tested in people, they can be tested in buildings by professionals or through do-it-yourself radon detection kits available in hardware and home supply stores (American Cancer Society, n.d.).

Short-term detection kits are left in place for several days, while long-term detection kits are left in place for three months before they are returned to a testing lab (American Cancer Society, n.d.).

While radon may be present anywhere, its level may be influenced by the characteristics of the rock and soil in the area (American Cancer Society, n.d.; U.S. Environmental Protection Agency, n.d.e). Its level may also be influenced by the floor level of the building. Units below the third floor may have higher levels, and basements may have the highest levels (American Cancer Society, n.d.; U.S. Environmental Protection Agency, n.d.d). Also, its level may be influenced by the presence of cracks in floors, walls, and construction joints or gaps in foundations around pipes, wires, and pumps (Allen & Macomber, 2020; U.S. Environmental Protection Agency, n.d.d). Strategies to lower radon levels are sealing cracks in floors and walls and increasing ventilation through pipes and fans (American Cancer Society, n.d.).

Maslow's Human Social Needs

In addition to the two physical needs specified in Maslow's hierarchy of human needs, there are *three social needs*. First, there is the *sense of belonging*, which may be achieved by having several people living in a home or neighbors who interact with each other in a community (Manturuk et al., 2017; Sassler & Miller, 2017). However, not all interactions lead to a sense of belonging, as domestic violence and neighborhood crime will cause distress (Austen, 2018; Botein & Hetling, 2016). The second social needs are *self-esteem or ego needs*, which may be realized by expressing one's image of self by buying or moving into a home that is recently rehabilitated or renovated or newly built, is spacious, has high-end amenities, or has an aesthetically pleasing interior and/or exterior design (Beamish & Goss, 2018). Finally, the third social need is *self-actualization*, which may be realized through creative expression in or around the home, such as through renovating, decorating, or gardening (Katz, 2009).

3.2 HOUSING AS A RIGHT

In contrast to the minimum, bottom, or "floor" perspective that regards housing as a basic need, there is a maximum, top, or "ceiling" perspective that regards the right to housing as an *aspirational ideal* embedded in many international human rights declarations, laws, and treaties, which, perhaps surprisingly, do not play a major role in U.S. housing policy discussions (Bratt et al., 2006). For example, Article 25 of the Universal Declaration of Human Rights, issued by the United Nations General Assembly on December 10, 1948, states the right to adequate housing as follows:

> [e]veryone has the right to a standard of living adequate for the health and well-being of himself and of his family, including food, clothing, housing and medical care and necessary social services, and the right to security in the event of unemployment, sickness, disability, widowhood, old age or other lack of livelihood in circumstances beyond his control.
>
> (United Nations, n.d., p. 7)

While the right to housing is an aspirational ideal in the U.S., adequate housing may be a more realistic goal (Bratt et al., 2006). The UN defines adequate housing as secure tenure (i.e., not being evicted from a home or land; United Nations Human Rights: Office of the High Commissioner, n.d.a). The right to adequate housing contains the following three types of freedoms:

> [p]rotection against forced evictions and the arbitrary destruction and demolition of one's home; [t]he right to be free from arbitrary interference with one's home, privacy and family; and [t]he right to choose one's residence, to determine where to live and to freedom of movement.
>
> (UNHABITAT, n.d., n.p.)

The right to housing also contains the following four entitlements: "security of tenure; [h]ousing, land[,] and property restitution; [e]qual and non-discriminatory access to adequate housing; [and p]articipation in housing-related decision-making at the national and community levels" (UNHABITAT, n.d., n.p.).

The Universal Declaration of the United Nations does not require the State to build housing for the entire population and does not grant housing to those without it. Rather, the right can be a system assuring the availability of decent affordable housing (Bull & Gross,

2023). However, the Declaration discusses efforts to prevent homelessness, prohibit forced evictions, address discrimination, ensure security of tenure, guarantee adequate housing, and focus on the most vulnerable groups (UNHABITAT, n.d.). These groups may consist of women, children, the homeless, persons with disabilities, displaced persons, migrants, refugees, and Indigenous peoples (Proctor, 2012). Also, the Declaration provides a legal basis that may help nonprofit organizations not only solve housing issues of individuals but influence their respective governments (Keating, 2020).

In addition to the aspirational goal and the efforts discussed in the Declaration, the United Nations has 44 thematic and 12 country Special Rapporteurs (SRs), who are independent experts appointed by the UN Human Rights Council (United Nations Human Rights: Office of the High Commissioner, n.d.b). These SRs make on-site visits, provide expertise, and respond to complaints, receiving staff and logistical assistance to undertake studies but no salary (American Civil Liberties Union, n.d.). One of the thematic SRs focuses "on adequate housing as a component of the right to an adequate standard of living, and on the right to non-discrimination in this context" (United Nations Human Rights: Office of the High Commissioner, n.d.a, n.p.). SR Leilani Farha, a trained lawyer who is the Executive Director of the NGO Canada Without Poverty, has served in this role since June 2014. Each thematic SR authors two annual reports, one for the General Assembly and one for the Human Rights Commission. The 2018 annual report to the General Assembly focused on the right to housing for residents of informal settlements, and the 2019 annual report to the Human Rights Commission discussed access to justice for the right to housing (United Nations Human Rights: Office of the High Commissioner, n.d.c, n.d.d).

4

HOUSING SUPPLY

Housing supply and building cycles are influenced by many factors, including the state of the economy, access to mortgages and mortgage interest rates, developer market assessments, community response, housing policy, and housing demand (the latter discussed in Chapter 5).

4.1 IMPACT ON HOUSING SUPPLY: STATE OF THE ECONOMY

The state of the economy may mean an economic expansion, which typically leads to an increase in housing construction, rehabilitation, and renovation activities, or it may mean an economic contraction or recession, determined by the National Bureau of Economic Research (NBER), which often leads to a decrease in these activities (Weber, 2015). As of this writing, the United States has gone through 12 recessions since the end of World War II (National Bureau of Economic Research, n.d.). Most recent recessions have occurred due to economic causes, including decreased spending by the government, firms, or consumers (as witnessed in many recessions); crashing financial markets (as witnessed in the recession that lasted from August 1929 to March 1933, also called the Great Depression); increasing energy prices (as seen in the recession that lasted from November 1973 to March 1975 due to the oil embargo of the Organization of Arab Petroleum Exporting Countries); or tightening monetary policies (as witnessed in the recession that lasted from July 1981 to November 1982, when the Federal Reserve fought inflation by raising interest rates; Bernanke, 2022; Bivens,

DOI: 10.1201/9781032657646-5

2019; Boushey & Shambaugh, 2019; Roberts, 2012). However, recessions may also occur due to public health crises, as seen in the most recent recession from February to April 2020, caused by the global COVID-19 pandemic (International Monetary Fund, 2020; National Bureau of Economic Research, n.d.).

The *Great Recession*, which lasted from December 2007 to June 2009, was somewhat unusual in terms of intensity, duration, and cause (Bernanke, 2015; Bernanke et al., 2020; National Bureau of Economic Research, n.d.). In terms of *intensity*, the impact of the Great Recession can be understood by looking at the gross domestic product (GDP), which is the total value of goods produced and services provided in a country during one year. The past ten recessions since the end of World War II, excluding the most recent one, had a cumulative GDP loss that ranged from 0.3% to 3.7%, while the Great Recession had a cumulative GDP loss of 4.1% (Anonymous, 2010a, 2010b). Similarly, the past ten recessions, also excluding the most recent one, had a loss in investment demand (i.e., business investment in plant and equipment and residential investment in home building) that ranged from 2.6% to 18.4%, while the Great Recession had a loss in investment demand of 23.4% (Anonymous, 2010a, 2010b).

In terms of *duration*, the past ten recessions, excluding the most recent one, had durations that ranged from six to 16 months, while the Great Recession lasted 18 months (Anonymous, 2010a; Hetzel, 2012). Whereas some past recessions were short-lived and had quick recoveries, such as the recessions that lasted from July 1990 to March 1991 and from March 2001 to November 2001, others were long-lived with slow recoveries, such as the recession that lasted from November 1973 to March 1975 and the Great Recession (Anonymous, 2010a, 2010b).

In terms of its *cause*, the Great Recession began when the supply of new homes began to outstrip demand in 2005, causing house prices to collapse after the spring of 2006 (CoreLogic, 2012; National Bureau of Economic Research, n.d.; Roubini & Mihm, 2011). In 2001, the Federal Reserve decreased interest rates to stimulate the economy during a mild recession (Barth, 2009). Thus, mortgage interest rates decreased and demand for homeownership increased, leading to increased house prices (Angell & Patel, 2017). Since the 1990s, lending standards had gradually decreased, as the financial industry actively pursued product innovation and pushed Congress for financial deregulation (Angell &

Patel, 2017). In this environment, many homebuyers, including some speculators, felt compelled to purchase a home before prices increased even further so they could lock in relatively low interest rates (Angell & Patel, 2017). At the same time, global institutional investors flooded the U.S. financial markets, creating pressure for the financial industry to create a relatively complex and opaque securitization process, design poorly understood derivative products, and leverage high-risk mortgages, all under the assumption that house prices would continue to increase (Barth, 2009). Indeed, from 2003 to 2007, average house prices increased by 38% (Leonard, 2022).

After house prices had started collapsing in the spring of 2006, borrowers with subprime mortgages (i.e., mortgages with a higher interest rate than prime or high quality mortgages) were unable to refinance their loans when interest rates reset upward in late 2006 and early 2007 (Anacker & Crossney, 2013). This inability to refinance primarily caused a national foreclosure crisis that started in early 2007 and peaked in 2009 and 2010, with foreclosure rates of 2.21% and 2.23% of all active loans, respectively, and foreclosure filings of about 2.82 million and 2.87 million, respectively (Angell & Patel, 2017). Thus, overall consumption declined nationally and portfolios with mortgage-related assets suffered catastrophic losses and liquidity shortages, revealing the interconnectedness, complexity, and the lack of transparency of the financial system (Angell & Patel, 2017). These crises gradually declined after 2011 (Attom Data Solutions, 2019).

Compared to non-Hispanic White and Asian borrowers, Black/African American and Hispanic/Latino borrowers disproportionately faced higher serious delinquency rates (i.e., missing monthly mortgage payments for 90 or more days) and higher foreclosure rates (i.e., having mortgages in the foreclosure process) during the Great Recession (Garriga et al., 2017). For example, Black/African American borrowers had a *delinquency* rate of 9.8% in January 2010, while the rate for Hispanic/Latino borrowers was 8.0%, Asian borrowers was 4.0%, and non-Hispanic White borrowers was 2.8% (Garriga et al., 2017). At the same time, Black/African American borrowers had a *foreclosure* rate of 28.6%, while the rate for Hispanic/Latino borrowers was 31.7%, Asian borrowers was 13.9%, and non-Hispanic White borrowers was 11.3% (Garriga et al., 2017).

The *national foreclosure crisis* that started in 2007 had repercussions on the national unemployment rate, which peaked at 10% in October 2009, twice the rate compared to 2007 and breaking the previous record rate that had been reached in 1983 (Boushey et al., 2019). Interestingly, the impact of the Great Recession was more severe for more vulnerable individuals in terms of race, ethnicity, and educational attainment. In terms of race and ethnicity, the unemployment rate was 15.8% for Blacks/African Americans, 12.8% for Hispanics/Latinos, 9.2% for non-Hispanic Whites, and 7.6% for Asians, based on data from the Bureau of Labor Statistics (S. Park, email correspondence, August 6, August 7, 2019). In terms of educational attainment, the unemployment rate was 14.8% for high school dropouts, 10.3% for high school graduates, 8.4% for people with some college experience, and 4.7% for people who had at least a Bachelor's degree (Boushey et al., 2019).

The NBER declared the end of the Great Recession in June 2009, although foreclosures and unemployment rates gradually declined in the early 2010s, as discussed above. However, the recovery from the Great Recession has been spatially uneven, such as in terms of house prices or vacancy rates (Crump & Schuetz, 2021). At the national level, median house prices increased by 9.8% from their "pre-recession peak value," possibly in 2005, to 2018, although there are differences among metropolitan areas and among ZIP codes *within* these metropolitan areas (Speakman, 2018, n.p.; the most recent information as of this writing). Indeed, some metropolitan areas (almost) fully recovered in terms of house prices, including Denver, Colorado; Austin, Texas; Dallas, Texas; San Antonio, Texas; and Seattle, Washington, among others (Speakman, 2018). These areas had relatively low foreclosure rates during the foreclosure crisis (Anacker, 2015b). Other metropolitan areas had large differences in *house price appreciation rates* among ZIP codes, including San Diego, Los Angeles, San Francisco, and San Jose, all considered booming housing markets in California (Speakman, 2018). For example, median home prices increased by 36.4% from "pre-recession peak value" to 2018 in San Francisco (Speakman, 2018). While 95.6% of homes in ZIP codes with low foreclosure rates recovered in terms of value, only 45.7% of homes in ZIP codes with high foreclosure rates did so (Speakman, 2018). Also, other metropolitan areas did not recover in terms of house prices at all, including Las Vegas, Nevada; Baltimore, Maryland; Riverside, California; and Orlando and Miami, both in Florida (Speakman, 2018). The metropolitan areas in this final group all had high foreclosure rates during the foreclosure crisis (Anacker, 2015b).

The recovery from the Great Recession has also been spatially uneven in terms of *vacancy rates*, which negatively impact residents' health, house prices, and neighborhood crime rates (Harrison & Immergluck, 2021). In the 200 largest metropolitan areas, vacancy rates decreased in Census tracts with a vacancy rate higher than 1% but increased in tracts with a vacancy rate lower than 1% from 2012 to 2019 (Harrison & Immergluck, 2021). However, vacancy rates increased in the Rust Belt (i.e., in states adjacent to the Great Lakes) in those tracts with a vacancy rate higher than 14% and with a rate lower than 1% (Harrison & Immergluck, 2021). By contrast, vacancy rates increased in the Sunbelt (i.e., in states partially or entirely south of the 37th parallel) in those tracts with a vacancy rate lower than 1% (Harrison & Immergluck, 2021). In sum, the recovery from the Great Recession has been spatially uneven and it will take years, if not decades, to bring most communities and individuals back to pre-Great Recession levels.

The most recent recession, which lasted from February to April 2020, was also unusual in terms of intensity, duration, and cause (National Bureau of Economic Research, n.d.). Although the GDP rapidly decreased by 10% during the second quarter of 2020 (compared to 4.1% during the Great Recession, as discussed above), it started bouncing back quickly in the third quarter of 2020, partly due to extensive recovery and relief programs, as discussed below (Center on Budget and Policy Priorities, 2023). This recession was caused by the global COVID-19 pandemic, triggered by an illness caused by a virus that spreads from person to person through respiratory droplets when an infected person coughs, sneezes, or talks, or when a person touches a surface or an object that has the virus on it and then touches their mouth, nose, or eyes, either causing no symptoms or mild to severe symptoms (Centers for Disease Control and Prevention, n.d.c).

Starting around mid-March 2020, the vast majority of U.S. governors issued stay-at-home orders to prevent both the spread of COVID-19 and an overload of the health care system by, for example, not allowing gatherings of groups over a certain size; closing recreational and entertainment businesses such as theaters, performing arts centers, concert venues, museums, barber shops, and public and private social clubs; and restricting nonessential businesses, such as restaurants, dining establishments, food courts, and farmers markets, to delivery and take-out services with adequate physical distancing (Commonwealth of Virginia, 2020).

Until December 2020, there was no vaccine or effective treatment against COVID-19 available (Centers for Disease Control and Prevention, n.d.c). Thus, people protected themselves by staying home to avoid close contact with others and wearing face masks that covered their nose and mouth in public, washing their hands often with soap and water for at least 20 seconds, staying physically distant from others, and various other mechanisms (Centers for Disease Control and Prevention, n.d.c). Older people and people of any age with serious underlying conditions were at higher risk for more serious illness, as evidenced in higher death rates (Centers for Disease Control and Prevention, n.d.d). While so-called nonessential workers (i.e., those who did not have to be on site) isolated themselves and worked from home, essential workers (i.e., those who had to be on site, including doctors and nurses, as well as grocery store and drugstore clerks) showed up for work and were thus exposed to the virus (Anacker, 2022). Thus, many in the latter group were infected with the virus, forcing them to isolate at home, and possibly lose their jobs (Ali et al., 2023). While the national umemployment rate was only 3.5% in February 2020, it was 14.8% in April 2020 (Bernanke, 2022).

Congress addressed the impacts of the COVID-19 pandemic by passing several Acts in 2020 and 2021 to address multiple anticipated challenges, including a nationwide wave of evictions and foreclosures. For example, Congress passed the *Families First Coronavirus Response Act* in mid-March 2020, which expanded emergency paid sick leave for employees who quarantined, were waiting on test results, were sick, or were taking care of their family members, although this expansion expired on December 31, 2020 (U.S. Department of Labor, n.d.a, n.d.b). This Act also provided temporary additional funding for existing food programs, including the Special Supplemental Nutrition Program for Women, Infants, and Children (WIC; these expanded benefits ended in December 2021) and the Supplemental Nutrition Assistance Program (SNAP; these expanded benefits ended in March 2023) (Rosenbaum et al., 2023; U.S. Department of Agriculture, n.d.b).

In late March 2020, Congress passed the *Coronavirus Aid, Relief, and Economic Security (CARES) Act*, intended to revive the cratering economy by assisting businesses and households, while continuing to address many anticipated challenges, including a nationwide wave of evictions and foreclosures (Barone, 2020). For example, many businesses, corporations, and state, local, and tribal governments obtained (forgivable) loans provided by the Paycheck Protection Program (PPP; Barone, 2020). However, more than 50% of these loans went to large companies (Leonard, 2022).

Households that had filed taxes in the previous year received a one-time cash payment (up to $1,200 for single adults, up to $2,400 for jointly-filing couples, depending on their incomes, and $500 per dependent child) (Alvarez & Steffen, 2021; Bernanke, 2022). Workers who had lost their job(s) received an additional $600 per week unemployment benefits (until July 26, 2020), and workers who had exhausted their unemployment benefits received them for an additional 13 weeks (Alvarez & Steffen, 2021; Barone, 2020; Leonard, 2022). In sum, the CARES Act and its December supplemental appropriations package were about 15% of the GDP in 2020 (Bernanke, 2022). In comparison, ARRA was more than 5% of the GDP in 2009 (Bernanke, 2022).

The CARES Act also protected select borrowers from foreclosure, granting forbearance (i.e., a pause or a reduction of but not forgiving payments) for a maximum of 18 months (Alexandrov et al., 2022; Consumer Financial Protection Bureau, n.d.). Eligible borrowers needed to have experienced hardship due to the pandemic and needed to have taken out a mortgage backed by the Federal National Mortgage Association (Fannie Mae), the Federal Home Loan Mortgage Corporation (Freddie Mac), the Federal Housing Administration (FHA), the U.S. Department of Veterans Affairs, and the U.S. Department of Agriculture (USDA; all discussed below) (Consumer Financial Protection Bureau, n.d.; Hepburn et al., 2021). While the CARES Act included an eviction moratorium for federally backed rental properties, it was not enforced, and it expired on July 24, 2020 (Eviction Lab, n.d.). The Centers for Disease Control and Prevention (CDC) then issued a nationwide eviction moratorium, effective from September 4, 2020 to July 31, 2021 (Eviction Lab, n.d.). In other words, housing providers were able to file eviction paperwork between July 25, 2020 and September 3, 2020 (Hepburn et al., 2021; Pendleton et al., 2021). Nevertheless, federal, state, and local eviction moratoria most likely prevented about 1.55 million evictions, although rents were not forgiven (Bull & Gross, 2023; Hepburn et al., 2021). However, on August 26, 2021, the U.S. Supreme Court ruled that the CDC had overstepped its authority by enforcing its moratorium, thus nullifying it (Eviction Lab, n.d.).

In mid-December 2020, Congress passed the *Consolidated Appropriations Act of 2021*, including the Coronavirus Response and Relief Supplemental Appropriations Act, 2021 (Division M) (Alvarez & Steffen, 2021). The latter Act continued the support for businesses, schools and universities, and state, local, and tribal governments, including the PPP (Associated Press, 2020). It also continued to support tax-filing households with an adjusted gross income of less than $75,000 through a one-time $600 stimulus check and unemployed households through extended federal unemployment benefits of $300 per week for up to 50 weeks (Alvarez & Steffen, 2021; Associated Press, 2020). U.S. Treasury administered the $25 billion Emergency Rental Assistance (ERA) program, benefitting states (Alvarez & Steffen, 2021).

Finally, in mid-March 2021, Congress passed the *American Rescue Plan Act of 2021*, again supporting businesses, schools, and state, local, and tribal governments, as well as eligible households (through a one-time payment of up to $1,400, as well as expanded tax credits for households with children) and unemployed households (through extended expanded unemployment benefits of $300 per week until September 6, 2021; Alvarez & Steffen, 2021; Bernanke, 2022; Cochrane, 2021). In sum, the American Rescue Plan Act funds were about 8% of the GDP in 2021 (Bernanke, 2022).

This Act also included rental, mortgage, and foreclosure prevention assistance programs for state and local governments, which provided grants to eligible households as well as expanded support for the homeless and other at-risk people (Cochrane, 2021; de la Campa & Reina, 2023; Hepburn et al., 2021). While these Acts and programs addressed many challenges during the COVID-19 pandemic, more than 1 million people had been killed by COVID-19 in the U.S. by April 2022 (Chappell, 2022). In late 2022, the U.S. government declared the COVID-19 pandemic to be over, although there were still communities with a high prevalence of the virus at that time (Chappell, 2022).

4.2 IMPACT ON HOUSING SUPPLY: ACCESS TO MORTGAGES AND MORTGAGE INTEREST RATES

Housing supply is influenced not only by economic recessions but also by *access to mortgages* and *mortgage interest rates*. From the late

1990s to the mid-2000s, it was relatively easy for most borrowers to access mortgages due to the ready availability of capital by international and domestic investors (Brown, 2015); the national house price bubble, fueled by irrational exuberance (Shiller, 2008); relatively low mortgage interest rates, facilitated by the Federal Reserve System (Freddie Mac, n.d.); the emergence of innovative mortgage products (Shiller, 2008); and relaxed paperwork requirements by some lenders (Shiller, 2008). Access to mortgages decreased during the Great Recession and has been low since (Goodman et al., 2020).

Access to mortgages may be indicated through several indices, such as the Housing Credit Availability Index (HCAI), among many others (Goodman et al., 2020). The HCAI, which is calculated by the Housing Finance Policy Center at the Urban Institute, assesses lenders' *ex ante* risk tolerance as exemplified by the proportion of mortgages for owner-occupied homes that are likely to become 90 or more days delinquent over the life of the loan (Goodman et al., 2020). A relatively high Index score indicates that lenders are indeed willing to tolerate borrower defaults, making it easier for borrowers to obtain a mortgage (Housing Finance Policy Center, 2019). In turn, a relatively low Index score indicates that lenders are unwilling to tolerate borrower defaults and thus may impose tighter lending standards, making it more difficult for borrowers to obtain a mortgage (Housing Finance Policy Center, 2019).

The HCAI peaked in the first quarter of 2006 at 16.77%, after the supply of new homes had begun to outstrip demand in 2005, causing house prices to start collapsing in the spring of 2006 (CoreLogic, 2012; National Bureau of Economic Research, n.d.). The HCAI bottomed out in the third quarter of 2013 at 4.57% due to uncertainty about those lenders that had sold mortgages to the government-sponsored enterprises (GSEs) Fannie Mae and Freddie Mac, which in turn bundled mortgages into securities guaranteed by the U.S. government and then sold these securities on the so-called secondary mortgage market (i.e., Wall Street), facilitating the flow of money into the housing market (Bernanke, 2022; Goodman et al., 2015). Interestingly, these lenders faced a repurchase risk in 2013, when the government retained the right to return the credit risk back to the lender if any mistakes in the underwriting of the mortgages were discovered, possibly leading to litigation by the U.S. Department of Justice (Goodman et al., 2015). Thus, during this time of uncertainty, lenders only originated loans to borrowers with pristine credit, resulting in a tight "credit box" (Goodman, 2017; Goodman et al., 2015; the most recent information as of this writing).

This constraint resulted in 1.25 million "missing loans" that could have been but were not made in 2013 (Goodman et al., 2019a, 2019b; Housing Finance Policy Center, 2019). Interestingly, racial and ethnic groups have been impacted differently by the "missing loans." For example, while the decline between 2001 and 2013 was 50.4% for Black/African American borrowers, it was 37.9% for Hispanic/Latino borrowers and 30.8% for non-Hispanic White borrowers, impacting homeownership and possibly wealth-building opportunities while reinforcing a severe racial and ethnic wealth gap (discussed below; Goodman et al., 2015). Interestingly, there was a small increase of 7.9% for Asian borrowers between 2001 and 2013 (Goodman et al., 2015). Although the Federal Housing Finance Agency (FHFA), the overseer of the GSEs, has clarified rules and regulations over the past several years, the HCAI only reached 4.7% in the fourth quarter of 2022, indicating that the "credit box" is still quite tight, which may be partially attributed to lower lender risk tolerance after the global COVID-19 pandemic (Urban Institute, n.d.).

Access to mortgages may also be influenced by *credit scores*, which signal lenders about a borrower's creditworthiness (i.e., how likely it is that they will pay back a loan, such as a mortgage or business loan or a credit card balance), based on their credit history recorded and maintained by the three credit bureaus Experian, Equifax, and TransUnion (Fair Isaac Corporation, n.d.a). Credit scores may also alert housing providers to the timeliness of rental payments of a future renter (Ratcliffe & Brown, 2017). The higher the credit score, the lower the risk to lenders (Fair Isaac Corporation, n.d.a).

In the U.S., the most common credit score is FICO® (Fair Isaac Corporation), ranging from 300 (poor rating) to 850 (exceptional rating; Fair Isaac Corporation, n.d.a). The Fair Isaac Company (FICO®) groups the FICO® score into the following clusters:

1. less than 580 (labeled "poor," well below the average score, possibly indicating a high risk);
2. between 580 and 669 ("fair," below the average score);
3. between 670 to 739 ("good," near or slightly above the average score);

4. between 740 and 799 ("very good," above the average score, possibly indicating dependability); and
5. above 800 ("exceptional," well above the average score, possibly indicating a very low risk).

(Fair Isaac Corporation, n.d.a)

FICO® scores predict the borrower's likelihood of honoring credit obligations and are utilized for preapproving credit (card) offers, approving credit (cards), setting credit terms, or changing credit lines on credit cards, among other uses (Fair Isaac Corporation, n.d.b). FICO® credit scores are calculated based on the following five components (Fair Isaac Corporation, n.d.b):

1. payment history (35% of the score);
2. amounts owed (30%);
3. length of credit history (15%);
4. new credit (10%); and
5. credit mix (10%).

Scores may be improved by checking one's credit report for errors, paying bills on time, reducing the amount of debt one owes, not opening many new accounts too rapidly, shopping for a loan within a limited period of time, re-establishing one's credit history if there were challenges, requesting and perusing one's credit report, applying and establishing new credit accounts only as needed, and managing credit cards responsibly (Fair Isaac Corporation, n.d.c).

As of August 2021, about 232 million people (almost 90%) of the total U.S. adult population (258 million people) were scorable, including 16.2 million who lost access to credit (i.e., people who may have encountered economic difficulties with a median age of 43 years), 7.4 million who FICO® calls "credit retired" (i.e., consumers who have not used credit over the past six months with a median age of 73 years), and 3.9 million who are new to credit (i.e., students, recent immigrants, and other active credit seekers with a median age of 23 years) (Fair Isaac Corporation, 2021a). There are also about 25 million (about 10%) without credit files, such as Generation Z members or millennials, or recent immigrants with a median age of 27 years (Fair Isaac Corporation, 2021a). As of May 2015, based on 2010 data and differentiating by neighborhood income, about 30% of adults were credit invisible (i.e., without any credit records at the three major credit bureaus) in low-income neighborhoods, in addition to about 15% of adults who were unscored (i.e., with credit records although these records were not sufficient to generate a score) (Brevoort et al., 2015). By contrast, in upper-income neighborhoods, about 4% of adults were credit invisible and about 5% were unscored (Brevoort et al., 2015, the most recent information as of this writing).

In order to increase the number of people in credit scoring, some companies have recently introduced scoring based on alternative data. For example, the FICO® Score XD includes expanded coverage that includes bill payment data, such as telecommunications, utility, retail, and rent payments (Fair Isaac Corporation, 2021b). The UltraFICO® Score contains consumer-contributed financial account data, such as information about checking, savings, and money market accounts (Fair Isaac Corporation, 2019; 2021b). Lastly, the FICO® Score 10 T includes trended credit bureau data (Wehrmann, 2022).

Although credit bureaus do not collect information on the race and ethnicity of borrowers, some researchers have nevertheless analyzed the number and proportion of consumers who are credit invisible or unscored. For example, Brevoort et al. (2015; the most recent information as of this writing) merged CFPB's Consumer Credit Panel (CCP) December 2010 data, which included longitudinal information on a sample of about 5 million de-identified credit records of an undisclosed credit bureau, and the 2010 Decennial Census data, as well as 2008–2012 American Community Survey (ACS) data for different racial and ethnic groups by tract. They found that 15% of Blacks/African Americans and Hispanics/Latinos, respectively, but only 9% of non-Hispanic Whites and Asians are credit invisible and that an additional 13% of Blacks/African Americans, 12% of Hispanics/Latinos, and 7% of non-Hispanic Whites are affected (Brevoort et al., 2015; the most recent information as of this writing).

Other researchers have combined data sets to analyze FICO® credit scores by race and ethnicity through analyses by, for example, combining the publicly available Home Mortgage Disclosure Act (HMDA) data set, housed by the Federal Financial Institutions Examination Council (FFIEC), with the proprietary CoreLogic mortgage servicing data set, among others (Goodman et al., 2015; Huynh, 2012). Results show a persistent racial and ethnic gap in FICO®

scores. For example, non-Hispanic White households had a median FICO® score of 752 in 2019, compared to Black/African American (694), Hispanic/Latino (714), and Asian households (763), illustrating continuing structural and individual challenges (Golding et al., 2021).

Housing supply is also influenced by *mortgage interest rates*, which are determined by multiple factors, including the benchmark interest rate set by the Federal Reserve's Federal Open Market Committee (FOMC), the inflation rate, the state of the job market, and the economy (Leonard, 2022; Lewis, 2023). Whereas mortgage interest rates were historically low until January 2022 (i.e., 3.2% for a 30-year fixed-rate mortgage, discussed below), they have increased recently since the COVID-19 pandemic to almost 7% in June 2023 (Lewis, 2023). This increase in mortgage interest rates means increased monthly mortgage payments that may lead to housing affordability challenges, as discussed below (Balsam & Gorman, 2023).

4.3 IMPACT ON HOUSING SUPPLY: DEVELOPER MARKET ASSESSMENTS, ZONING, AND COMMUNITY RESPONSE

In addition to the state of the economy, access to mortgages, and mortgage *interest rates*, housing supply is also influenced by *developer market assessments*, *zoning*, and *community response*. In the United States, the vast majority of housing construction is undertaken by for-profit and nonprofit developers, some of them possibly assisted by intermediaries such as the Enterprise Community Partners, which channels private, socially conscious, performance-based capital investment to underinvested communities, among many other activities (Enterprise Community Partners, n.d.). Only a very small proportion of housing construction, but a somewhat larger proportion of housing rehabilitation and renovation, is coordinated or undertaken by homeowners themselves, which either hire a contractor or invest "sweat equity," possibly utilizing second-hand construction materials (Harris, 1996, 2012; U.S. Department of Agriculture, n.d.a).

Developers constantly monitor markets, as expressed by the National Association of Home Builders (NAHB) Wells Fargo Housing Market Index (HMI) (National Association of Home Builders, n.d.). The HMI is based on a monthly survey of NAHB members, who assess market conditions for the sale of new homes as well as the interest of prospective buyers in new homes at present and over the next six months (National Association of Home Builders, n.d.). The Index is a weighted average of three subindices that ranges from 0, indicating very poor market conditions, to 100, indicating excellent market conditions. For example, in January 2009, when the U.S. was in the middle of the Great Recession, the Index was 8, whereas in December 1998, when the U.S. was in the middle of an economic boom, the Index was 78 (National Association of Home Builders, n.d.). In June 2023, the Index was 55, indicating that the responding NAHB members assessed market conditions as satisfactory (National Association of Home Builders, n.d.).

Zoning also impacts housing supply. Zoning occurs when a municipality designates different land uses to separate areas and then enforces a particular land use (Levy, 2006). New York City passed the Building Zone Resolution in 1916, triggered by the construction of the massive 36-story-high Equitable Building at 120 Broadway in 1914, which not only cast a large shadow over more than one block and emitted smoke, steam, odors, and noise, but also generated high foot traffic, especially during the lunch hour, when people enjoyed their breaks (Revell, 2003; Wallace, 2017). Others argue that the Resolution was influenced by merchants on Fifth Avenue, who were concerned about the rapidly expanding Garment District, with its densely packed buildings (Berg, 2018; Johnson, D. A., 1996). Others observed that homeowners were concerned about businesses and manufacturers moving into their neighborhoods (Fogelson, 2001). New York City's 1916 Building Zone Resolution led the United States Department of Commerce, from 1921 to 1926, to draft and eventually finalize the Standard State Zoning Enabling Act, which provided states a template for passing their own zoning enabling laws (Levy, 2006). The U.S. Supreme Court upheld the constitutionality of zoning based on *Village of Euclid, Ohio v. Ambler Reality Co* in 1926 (Levy, 2006).

Exclusionary zoning may occur when there are building restrictions, such as minimum lot sizes or square footages, height limits, or building type restrictions, such as prohibiting the construction of multifamily homes (Rouse et al., 2021). An example of exclusionary zoning occurred in Mount Laurel, a suburban township in southern New Jersey, when the township evicted Black/African American families from substandard housing in the 1960s (Mallach, 2012).

Some community members asked the township to rezone a nearby area, allowing affordable housing, but officials refused (Mallach, 2012). In turn, some evicted families turned to the NAACP, which sued the township in 1971 (*Southern Burlington County NAACP et al. v. Township of Mount Laurel*) (Mallach, 2012). A year later, the judge ordered the township to pass an affordable housing plan, benefitting its low-income residents (Mallach, 2012). However, the township appealed, leading the New Jersey Supreme Court to decide that municipalities have a "constitutional obligation to provide for their fair share of the regional need for affordable housing" (Mount Laurel I) (Mallach, 2012, p. 483). Nevertheless, most municipalities ignored this decision until 1983, when Chief Justice Robert Wilentz issued an opinion that included a so-called builder's remedy. In this case, builders that had proposed developments with a significant percentage of units geared toward low- and moderate-income residents but were turned down in municipalities that had failed to meet their fair share of affordable housing were eligible for redress from the courts (Mount Laurel II) (Mallach, 2012). In other words, courts could mandate municipalities to issue remedial measures, including issuing building permits for developments with a percentage of affordable units (Mallach, 2012). These two Mount Laurel decisions have impacted land use and affordable housing not only in New Jersey but also in other municipalities nationwide.

Inclusionary zoning has the goal of expanding the local or regional affordable housing supply, facilitating long-term housing affordability (Anacker, 2020). It may occur when local governments in states that grant them the power to adopt policies, such as Maryland or Virginia, require developers to include a certain number or proportion of affordable housing units in new residential developments (Cowan, 2006). Inclusionary zoning may also occur when local governments in states that have the authority to determine the regional need for affordable housing, such as California or New Jersey, are allocated a fair share of affordable housing to them, which they then have to implement, as discussed above in the case of New Jersey (Cowan, 2006).

Inclusionary housing may be funded by or through local Community Development Corporations (CDCs), housing trust funds, developer impact fees, real estate transaction fees, state or local property tax levies, dedicated sales and use taxes, tax increment financing

(TIF), and bond financing. CDCs are nonprofit, community-based organizations that were established in the late 1960s/early 1970s to address community challenges such as job training, commercial revitalization, dilapidated or affordable housing, (the lack of) public services, and crime (Bull & Gross, 2023; Keating, 2012). CDCs typically obtain funding through federal, state, and local governments or foundations (Bull & Gross, 2023; Keating, 2012).

Housing trust funds, regardless of whether they are established or administered at the federal, state, or local level, receive annual budget allocations to preserve or produce affordable housing (Housing Trust Fund Project, n.d.). TIFs are financing tools based on a local or regional redevelopment agency, which issues bonds, the proceeds of which finance developments where property values are projected to increase (Fisher & Leite, 2018). While the base goes to the original taxing authority, the increase pays off development costs (Fisher & Leite, 2018). Inclusionary housing may be promoted by several programs, including the Low Income Housing Tax Credit (LIHTC) program, the Community Development Block Grants (CDBG) program, the HOME Investment Partnerships Program, all discussed below (Anacker, 2020). Inclusionary housing may also be linked to the Housing Choice Voucher (HCV) Program, also discussed below (Anacker, 2020). As of 2018/2019, there were 1,019 local inclusionary housing programs in 734 jurisdictions in 31 states and Washington, DC (Wang & Balachandran, 2023). The most inclusionary housing programs were in New Jersey (222; 30.2% of all programs), followed by California (162; 22.1%), Massachusetts (140; 19.1%), New York (36; 4.9%), and Florida (23; 3.1%) (Wang & Balachandran, 2023).

Community response may occur whenever there is a change to the building stock in a neighborhood, including when plans for a newly constructed, rehabilitated, or repurposed building, sometimes called "infill housing," are revealed. These could be affordable homes, halfway houses, or homeless shelters, all of which might lead homeowners to fear a negative impact on their health, their property values, or neighborhood safety or traffic (McCabe, 2016). Community response may also occur when there is a visual offense or imminent danger, such as when a building is considered an eyesore or an abandoned building is about to collapse, but it is not addressed (Kinder, 2016). Community response may be labeled "not in my backyard," or NIMBY, indicating relatively strong property rights and the power of voting homeowners (Fischel, 2001, 2015; Massey et al., 2013; Prevost, 2013).

The state of the economy, access to mortgages and mortgage interest rates, developer market assessments, zoning, community response, and housing policy, among others, influence *housing construction*, which may be exemplified by the number of issued building permits and the number of housing units started and completed, typically regarded as a bellwether of the economy (Bull & Gross, 2023) (see Figure 4.1). For example, just before the national house price bubble burst in 2005, the number of permits issued (2.155 million) and the number of housing units started (2.068 million) and completed (1.931 million) peaked (U.S. Bureau of the Census, n.d.a). By contrast, when the Great Recession bottomed in 2009, the number of permits issued (about 583,000) and the number of housing units started (about 554,000) and completed (about 794,000) were decreases of approximately 72%, 73%, and 59%, respectively (U.S. Bureau of the Census, n.d.a).

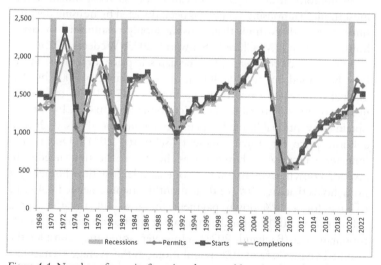

Figure 4.1 Number of permits for privately owned housing issued, and number of housing units started and completed, 1968–2022

Source: author, based on U.S. Bureau of the Census (n.d.a.).

While developer market assessment bottomed out in January 2009 and the credit box tightened until 2013 and only gradually relaxed over time, the foreclosure crisis peaked around 2010, leading to a large number of Real Estate Owned (REO) properties in many communities (Attom Data Solutions, 2019). These were properties where the owners/borrowers had been unable to make monthly mortgage payments for 90 or more days and thus the lenders evicted them and repossessed the properties while trying to find new residents (Dayen, 2016). Since many potential buyers were affected by the Great Recession, most of them were unable to obtain mortgages (Dayen, 2016). Some potential renters were unable to afford the rents of the repossessed homes (Dayen, 2016). Thus, many REOs remained vacant and needed to be boarded up and secured to prevent scalping and squatting, thus further reducing housing supply (Kinder, 2016).

Since 2009, *housing construction* has rebounded and increased, as exemplified by the number of permits issued (1.67 million) and the number of housing units started (1.55 million) and completed (1.39 million) in 2022 (U.S. Bureau of the Census, n.d.a). While most think that housing supply has been dwarfed by housing demand since 2009, others think that housing supply is sufficient to satisfy housing demand (McClure & Schwartz, 2023; Wedeen, 2023).

In the case of *house prices*, the median sale price for a home in the U.S. bottomed out at $208,400 in the first quarter of 2009 but has gradually increased since then, peaking at $479,500 in the fourth quarter of 2022 (Federal Reserve Economic Data, n.d.a). In order to obtain conventional home financing, borrowers need to save 20% of a home price for down payment (Schwartz, 2021). Due to the long-term increase in home prices, however, the time needed to save for a down payment is long. For example, first-time homebuyer households that save 10% of their monthly income needed 6.4 years to save for a 20% down payment for a so-called starter home ($148,527) in 2021, defined as a home at the bottom third of a metropolitan area (Bachaud, 2021). However, some may consider the assumed savings rate of 10% as ambitious, as the average savings rate of renter households has been around 2.4% over the past two decades or so (Parrott & Zandi, 2021). Also, the number of years to save for a 20% down payment for a starter home is high in coastal metropolitan areas, with 17.9 years in San Diego, 17.6 years in Los Angeles,

17.4 years in San Francisco, 13.0 years in Boston, and 11.7 years in New York in 2021 (Bachaud, 2021).

In terms of *race and ethnicity*, the time to save for a down payment is higher for many Blacks/African Americans and Hispanics/Latinos due to the severe racial and ethnic wealth gap (Dettling et al., 2017; Shapiro, 2017). For example, non-Hispanic White households had a median wealth of $188,200 compared to Hispanic/Latino ($36,100) and Black/African American ($24,100) households in 2019, illustrating continued structural and individual challenges (Bhutta et al., 2020; the most recent information as of this writing). At the national level, a non-Hispanic White renter with a median income needed about six years and one month to save for a 20% down payment on a starter home, compared to an Asian renter who needed about four years and six months, a Black/African American renter who needed about nine years and seven months, and a Hispanic/Latino renter who needed about seven years and eight months (Bachaud, 2021). Similar to the gender gap, the racial and ethnic gap may take several decades to close (Asante-Muhammed et al., 2016).

In sum, the state of the economy, access to mortgages and mortgage interest rates, developer market assessments, zoning, and community response, along with *individual preferences and responses, subtle and overt discrimination*, and *weak government enforcement*, may lead to *job and housing imbalances. Job imbalances* may cause some workers to move to distant, more affordable neighborhoods, as they may not be able to afford living in closer neighborhoods (Jacobus, 2015). This contributes to traffic congestion and high expenditures on transportation by those workers who have to be on site, including first responders such as paramedics, emergency medical technicians, police officers, firefighters, and rescuers, as well as other essential professionals, such as public school teachers (Myerson, 2016). Job imbalances may contribute to local (essential) worker shortages, air pollution, taxpayer expenditures, and sprawl (Jacobus, 2015).

Housing imbalances may lead to concentrations of low-income households in low-opportunity neighborhoods, resulting in *economic, racial, and ethnic residential segregation* (Dougherty, 2021; Jacobus, 2015; Quart, 2018). Segregation may lead to unequal access to high-quality grocery stores, places of employment, schools, health care, financial and retail facilities, and green spaces (Anacker et al., 2017). For some households and individuals, segregation may result in nutritional challenges, unemployment and underemployment, low incomes, low school test scores, health challenges, and being unbanked, underbanked, or underserved (Baradaran, 2015; Lopez, 2012; Millstone & Lang, 2013; Servon, 2017; Wherry et al., 2019). In addition, segregation may result in fortified stereotypes and racism (Bull & Gross, 2023).

5

HOUSING DEMAND

Housing demand is influenced by many factors, including:

- population and its life expectancy;
- household income;
- household size;
- family lifecycle stage and multigenerational households;
- access to mortgages (see Chapter 6); and
- housing policy (see Chapters 7, 8, 9, and 10).

5.1 IMPACT ON HOUSING DEMAND: POPULATION AND LIFE EXPECTANCY

Over the past several decades, the United States has witnessed a large increase in its *population*, from about 151 million in 1950, to 281 million in 2000, to 308 million in 2010, and it is projected to reach 404 million by 2060 (U.S. Bureau of the Census, n.d.b; Vespa et al., 2020). By 2030, international migration is projected to surpass the natural population increase (i.e., births minus deaths), although these projections were influenced by current and future immigration policies that are unfolding, as of this writing (Vespa et al., 2020). In sum, the past, current, and future large increases in population may translate into a large increase in housing demand over the next few years and decades.

DOI: 10.1201/9781032657646-6

Over the past several decades, *life expectancy* in the U.S. continuously increased until 2019. Whereas life expectancy at birth was 47 years in 1900, regardless of sex and race, it peaked at almost 79 years in 2019 due to rapid reductions in infant and early childhood mortality at the beginning of the 20th century (Shmerling, 2022). It also peaked because of declining mortality, particularly heart disease, in late age during the last third of the 20th century due to medical advances, behavioral changes, lower rates of smoking, and overall improvements in the quality of life (Anonymous, 2016; Olshansky et al., 2012).

However, life expectancy had *increased differently by sex, race, and ethnicity*. With regard to sex, life expectancy at birth was 46.3 years for males but 48.3 years for females in 1900, or a difference of two years, and then it was 76.3 years for males and 81.4 years for females in 2019, or a difference of 5.1 years (Arias et al., 2021; Centers for Disease Control and Prevention, 2017; National Center for Health Statistics, 2022). The reasons for higher female life expectancy are inherent biological advantages, as well as behavioral differences, such as lower rates of smoking and alcohol use, among others (World Health Organization, n.d.).

With regard to race and ethnicity, life expectancy at birth was 47.6 years for Whites and 33 years for Blacks in 1900, or a difference of 14.6 years, but it was 78.8 years for non–Hispanic Whites and 74.7 years for Blacks/African Americans in 2019, or a difference of 4.1 years (Arias et al., 2021; Centers for Disease Control and Prevention, 2017; the most recent information as of this writing). Similarly, life expectancy at birth was 78.8 years for non-Hispanic Whites, 74.7 years for Blacks/African Americans, and 81.8 years for Hispanics/Latinos in 2019, with a positive difference of 4.1 years between non-Hispanic Whites and Blacks/African Americans and a negative difference of 3 years between non-Hispanic Whites and Hispanics/Latinos (Arias et al., 2021; Centers for Disease Control and Prevention, 2017). The difference in life expectancy at birth between non-Hispanic Whites and Blacks/African Americans can be attributed to a relatively low average number of years spent in education and an average lower socioeconomic status for many Blacks/African Americans, including lower incomes, physically demanding occupations, and a lack of access to health care (Olshansky et al., 2012). The difference in life expectancy at birth between non-Hispanic Whites and Hispanics/ Latinos can be attributed to the mortality rate of immigrant Hispanics/Latinos, which is 10–20% lower than that of U.S.-born Hispanics/Latinos, as well as to the fact that Hispanic/Latino immigrants are often in better health and have better educated than people who do not emigrate, which is called "health selection" (Olshansky et al. 2012, p. 1805; Wilkerson, 2020).

While life expectancy at birth has increased over the past decades, it declined in 2020 due to the COVID-19 pandemic and drug overdoses, which contributed to the largest decrease over two years since the 1920s (Murphy et al., 2018; Shmerling, 2022; Wilkerson, 2020; Xu et al., 2022). In 2021, the top 10 causes of death, based on the number of deaths per 100,000 population, were heart disease, cancer, COVID-19, unintentional injuries, stroke, chronic lower respiratory diseases, Alzheimer's disease, diabetes, chronic liver disease and cirrhosis, and kidney disease (Xu et al., 2022). From 2000 to 2019, the rates of many causes of death had decreased over time, including heart disease; cancer; chronic lower respiratory diseases; stroke; diabetes; influenza and pneumonia; and nephritis, nephrotic syndrome, and nephrosis. These decreases may be attributed to improved behavior, increased (access to) health care, and possibly better affordability of health care due to national health care reform in the early 2010s (Xu et al., 2022).

Interestingly, the rates of some causes of death increased from 2020 to 2021, including 22.5% for COVID-19, 12.3% for unintentional injuries, 9% for chronic liver disease and cirrhosis, 7.1% for kidney disease, 5.9% for stroke, 3.3% for heart disease, 2.4% for diabetes, and 1.7% for cancer (Xu et al., 2022). The increase in the rate of unintentional injuries may be attributed to an increased number of falls due to increased longevity and an increased number of poisoning accidents due to drug, and especially opioid, overdoses among adults, as well as poisoning from medicines and household cleaners among children (Centers for Disease Control and Prevention, n.d.b; Xu et al., 2022). While the global COVID-19 pandemic has officially been declared over, it remains to be seen whether the rate of unintentional injuries, including opioid overdoses, will decrease the number and proportion of "deaths of despair" and thus increase life expectancy again, which may translate into an increase in housing demand over time (Case & Deaton, 2021).

5.2 IMPACT ON HOUSING DEMAND: HOUSEHOLD INCOME

Housing demand may also be influenced by *household income*. Over the past four decades, national real household incomes (i.e., incomes adjusted for inflation) have generally increased during economic expansions but decreased just before and during economic recessions (see Figure 5.1). For example, real household incomes peaked at $61,153 in 1989, declined just before the recession that lasted from July 1990 to March 1991, bottomed out at $57,843 in 1993 once the economy went into recovery, peaked at $66,385 in 1999, declined just before the recession that lasted from March 2001 to November 2001, again bottomed out at $60,313 in 2012, then increased to $72,808 in 2019, and decreased to $70,784 in 2021 (Federal Reserve Economic Data, n.d.b; see Figure 5.1). While increased household incomes may mean more choices on the housing market for some, these increased incomes may not necessarily be sufficient, given rapidly increasing house prices and rents, as discussed above.

Earnings are determined by many factors, including education and experience levels; skill levels; professional sectors, including the perception of whether a sector is perceived as female (e.g., health care

Figure 5.1 Real median household incomes, 1984–2021

Source: author, based on Federal Reserve Economic Data (n.d.b).

and professional services, clerical and sales jobs) versus male (e.g., construction and architectural services); achievements and productivity; the degree of unionization; age, gender, racial, ethnic, and nativity discrimination (or the lack of it); females being perceived as prioritizing childcare and eldercare; professional networks, including so-called weak ties; and possibly luck (Anacker, 2022; Granovetter, 1973; Mishel et al., 2012: Wilkerson, 2020).

However, there are racial and ethnic differences. Since the early 2000s, Asians have had the highest real median household incomes, followed by non-Hispanic Whites, Hispanics/Latinos, and Blacks/African Americans. For example, non-Hispanic Asian households earned $94,903 in 2020, followed by non-Hispanic White households ($74,912), Hispanic/Latino households ($55,321), and Black/African American households ($45,870; U.S. Bureau of the Census, n.d.e.; see Figure 5.2). Furthermore, there are also gender differences. For example, median hourly earnings of female full- and part-time workers were only 82% of the earnings of male workers in 2022, compared to 80% in 2002 (Aragão, 2023). While this gap has narrowed slightly over the past twenty years, it may take several decades to close it (Institute for Women's Policy Research, 2017; the most recent information as of this writing).

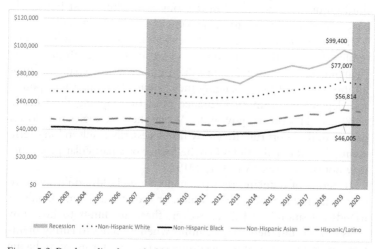

Figure 5.2 Real median household incomes by race and ethnicity, 2002–2020

Source: author, based on U.S. Bureau of the Census (n.d.e).

Households can respond to real household income decline by increasing household incomes and decreasing household expenditures. Households may increase household incomes by sending additional earners into the workforce and finding employment with higher salaries. However, labor participation may have already been exhausted by many households, as the day has only 24 hours, there are limited numbers of workers in each household, all teenage and adult household members may have already entered the workforce, or there may be a skills mismatch (i.e., workers do not have the skills that the labor market needs; Anacker, 2019). Finding employment with higher salaries may be difficult, as some employees may be forced to move to an area with a higher cost of living or face longer commutes, which may translate into increased household expenses, thus annihilating a potentially increased household income (Anacker, 2019).

In addition to increasing household incomes, households may decrease household expenditures. First, they may decrease somewhat fixed expenditures, such as health care premia and rent and mortgage payments. Second, they may decrease less flexible expenditures, such as transportation to work, health care expenditures, child care, and utility expenditures. Third, they may decrease more flexible expenditures, such as food and clothing. While expenditures that fall into the first two groups have increased, expenditures that fall into the third group have decreased in the long run. Thus, most household have had reduced room to maneuver (Warren & Tyagi, 2003).

In terms of somewhat fixed expenditures, households could reduce their health care premia by changing their health insurance, changing to less expensive health insurance plans, changing their locations of residence, changing their habits, dropping their spouses and dependents from an insurance plan, or dropping their health insurance (HealthCare.gov, n.d.). While these strategies may lower premia in the short run, they may not necessarily result in long-term savings because deductibles may be higher or a particular procedure may not be covered (Anacker, 2019).

In terms of reducing rent payments, households could move to units with lower rents, sublet rooms, or "couch surf" with family or friends (Desmond, 2016). However, there are limits to how low rents can go, and there may be limits when it comes to family members or friends providing accommodation. In terms of reducing mortgage payments, households could negotiate mortgage terms to achieve lower monthly mortgage payments, assuming that the lender will cooperate (Anacker, 2019).

In terms of less flexible expenditures, households could reduce expenditures for transportation to work, health care, child care, and utilities. For example, households could take public transportation, ride bikes, or walk instead of driving cars. However, public transportation may not be available or only be available during unneeded hours, may entail longer travel times, or may require changing between or among different transportation modes (Kneebone & Berube, 2013). Alternatives may be working from home or an alternative location close to home, although only some workers may have this option (Muro et al., 2017). Thus, households may find it difficult to reduce transportation expenditures.

Households may decrease health care expenditures (apart from health care premia) by skipping or stretching out medications or doctors' exams or tests, which may be unhealthy and unsustainable in the long term (Correspondents of *The New York Times*, 2005). Households may forego child care expenditures by not having children or relying on family members and friends to provide services for free or in exchange for other services (Edin & Shaefer, 2016). Child care expenditures may be decreased by requesting child care services in facilities that are less expensive (Abramsky, 2013). However, facilities may be further from homes or workplaces, adding to commuting expenses and time, or they may offer lower quality services, resulting in other potential expenditures in the mid or long term (Harrington, 2012). Households may decrease expenditures by signing up for a reduced number of hours of child care services, which may decrease the number of hours worked and thus decrease salaries (Edelman, 2013).

Utility services (e.g., water, sewerage, power or gas, heating, and air conditioning) are typically needed to live comfortably. Households may reduce or even forego these expenses by living in a housing unit that is geared toward saving on utility expenses, although this may result in higher rents and home values (and thus higher mortgage payments). Households may also defer these expenses by not paying their bills, although only until the utilities are shut off (Morduch & Schneider, 2017). For the most part, less flexible expenditures are difficult to decrease.

Finally, there are several examples of more flexible expenditures that have some room to decrease (Warren & Tyagi, 2003). For example, households may save on food expenditures by foregoing eating out and ordering takeout food, eating less expensive food, reducing food portions, skipping meals, visiting food pantries, or begging (Edin & Shaefer, 2016). Households may save on clothing expenditures by wearing outfits longer, buying or receiving clothing second hand, or making their own clothing (Edin & Schaefer, 2016). Generally, more flexible expenditures may be less difficult to decrease. While increasing household incomes and decreasing household expenditures may sound like strategies typically utilized by many low-income households, Cohen (2017) and Morduch and Schneider (2017) show that the aftermath of the Great Recession has also affected many middle-income households that also utilize these strategies.

5.3 IMPACT ON HOUSING DEMAND: HOUSEHOLD SIZE

Housing demand is also influenced by the average *household size*, which has gradually decreased over the past few decades. An increased population living in households with fewer people translates into an increased demand for housing (Kislev, 2019). The average household size decreased from 3.33 in 1960, to 3.14 in 1970, to 2.76 in 1980, to 2.63 in 1990, to 2.62 in 2000, to 2.59 in 2010, and then to 2.53 in 2020 (U.S. Bureau of the Census, n.d.d). Over the past several decades, the proportion of single-person households has increased from 13% in 1960 to 28% in 2020 (36.2 million households; U.S. Bureau of the Census, 2018). In turn, the proportion of households with married couples has decreased from 75% in 1960 to 48% in 2020 (62.3 million households; U.S. Bureau of the Census, n.d.d.).

The reasons for the increase in single-person households are Social Security, whose benefits may enable some retirees to live on their own instead of moving in with family; increased rates of workforce participation among females, which may mean a career focus along with career-related moves; urbanization and the increase in third places; the increase in longevity, which may mean that some people remain single after their spouses die; and an increasing focus on freedom, flexibility, individualism, and personal choice (Klinenberg, 2012; Ocejo, 2017).

Research conducted in the mid-1990s projected an average household size of 2.53 instead of the actual 2.59 in 2010 (Day, 1996; Nelson, 2013). This slower than projected decrease of average household size may be attributed to the Great Recession, including the national foreclosure crisis and its record-high unemployment rate, which caused many people to move (back) in with their family or friends, including evicted homeowners and renters, as well as college graduates who were unable to find full-time, well-paying jobs that would have enabled them to form their own households (Bureau of Labor Statistics, n.d.a; Sullivan, 2018).

While the national foreclosure crisis has gradually ended and the national labor market had gradually recovered by the mid-2010, some households have not recovered in terms of their budgets, and some workers have not found jobs that would enable them to form households (Cohen, 2017; Morduch & Schneider, 2017). Also, the national unemployment rate only includes people who are available for work in the first place and who have actively looked for work in the prior four weeks (Bureau of Labor Statistics, n.d.b). Thus, many people may not be included in this rate. Furthermore, there are vast differences in the unemployment rate by age, race, and ethnicity. In terms of age, the 2022 unemployment rate was 7.0% for people between 20 and 24 years compared to 3.1% for people between 25 and 54 years (Bureau of Labor Statistics, n.d.a). In terms of race and ethnicity, the 2021 unemployment rate was 4.7% for non-Hispanic Whites, 8.6% for Blacks/African Americans, 5.0% for Asians, and 6.8% for Hispanics/Latinos (Bureau of Labor Statistics, n.d.a). These factors may impact household size.

5.4 IMPACT ON HOUSING DEMAND: FAMILY LIFECYCLE STAGES AND MULTIGENERATIONAL HOUSEHOLDS

Furthermore, housing demand is influenced by the *family lifecycle stages* (i.e., maturation, generation, and decline) that households go through over their lifetime, assuming a heterosexual couple with an intact marriage and children over the couple's lifetime (Beamish & Goss, 2018). During these family lifecycle stages, there may be single young adults who leave the home, new couples who establish families through marriage, nuclear families with young children, families with adolescents, families who launch children and move on, and couples who are in later life (Carter & McGoldrick, 1989). While this differentiation may still be valid for some households, it does not include households that stay single, remain childless, cohabitate, divorce, remarry, blend households, or become widowed at an early age (Newman, 2012).

Housing demand is also influenced by *multigenerational households* (i.e., two related adults from different generations living under one roof), which may be formed by parents moving in with their adult children or grandchildren, adult children or grandchildren moving in with their parents or grandparents, and many other combinations (Pfeiffer et al., 2016). In 2021, 18% of the population (or almost 60 million) lived in multigenerational households, up from 12.7% (or about 26 million) in 1970 (Cohn et al., 2022). Multigenerational households were more common among Blacks/African Americans and Hispanics/Latinos (both at 26%), followed by Asians (24%) and non-Hispanic Whites (13%); among people ages 25–39 and 55–64 (both at 22%), followed by people over 85 (at 20%); and among people who are foreign-born (26%) compared to native-born (17%; Cohn et al., 2022).

The gradual increase in multigenerational households may be attributed to demographic and cultural factors. There has been an increase in longevity over the past few decades, which typically coincides with health-related issues (Kislev, 2019). Furthermore, there has been an increase in the number and proportion of single, divorced, or widowed childless, younger adult females, who have higher odds of living in multigenerational households (Pilkauskas, 2012; Ruggles, 2007). The increase in the number of shared years lived between and among generations has resulted in the so-called "sandwich generation" (i.e., middle-aged adults with aging parents and children), who may have double caretaking responsibilities (Parker & Patten, 2013).

In terms of *cultural factors*, caretaking responsibilities for some grandparents and other family members have increased due to the increased rates of female workforce participation, marital instability, cohabitation, divorce, and widowhood over the past few decades (Taylor, 2014). Hispanics/Latinos, Blacks/African Americans, and Asians are more likely to live in multigenerational households than non-Hispanic Whites. For example, some Hispanics/Latinos may combine households because of fewer resources but higher needs, a focus on families and filial obligations, preference for informal care arrangements over institutionalized care, language barriers and degree of acculturation, recent immigration and the five-year waiting period for access to welfare benefits, and a relatively high proportion of immigrants with an uncertain migration status (Taylor, 2014).

Some Blacks/African Americans may live in multigenerational households due to the intergenerational support networks that are needed when there are fewer economic resources but higher needs; higher rates of single mothers; higher teenage pregnancy rates; higher rates of disability; and a higher degree of household challenges, including incarceration rates, compared to other racial and ethnic groups (Alexander, 2012; Harris, 2016).

Many Asians may live in multigenerational households due to a tradition of filial responsibility, which is derived from Confucianism, Buddhism, or Islamism (i.e., absolute love and respect for one's parents and ancestors, especially along the male line). Asian multigenerational households also form because of language barriers and fewer resources (Taylor, 2014).

As the numbers and proportions of Asians and Hispanics are projected to increase, the number and proportion of multigenerational households will most likely increase as well, in particular in suburbs in the Sunbelt South and the Western U.S. (Lung-Amam, 2020). Taylor Morrison, the Lennar Corporation, and Toll Brothers are all national homebuilders that have specialized in multigenerational homes that include self-contained suites, indicating that there is demand for such housing (Lung-Amam, 2020). Therefore, it remains to be seen if and by how much the average household size might decrease in the near and distant future.

Since generations have different characteristics, including their housing demand, researchers have differentiated among the following four generational groups: (1) the *millennial generation* (born between 1981 and 1996); (2) *Generation X* (born between 1965 and 1980); (3) the *baby boomer generation* (born between 1946 and 1964); and (4) the *silent generation* (born between 1928 and 1945; Fry, 2020). As of 2020, the largest group was the millennial generation (about 72.1 million), followed by the baby boomer generation (about 71.6 million), and Generation X (about 65.2 million) (Fry, 2020; the most recent information as of this writing). The millennial generation is projected to grow due to the influx of young immigrants, and Generation X is projected to be larger than the baby boomer generation in 2028, as members of the latter group age and eventually die (Fry, 2020; the most recent information as of this writing).

These generational groups have different housing demands. For example, some members of the millennial and silent generations may appreciate living in small, maintenance-free apartments or low-maintenance condominiums in walkable neighborhoods with access to public transportation, grocery stores, and third places (Oldenburg, 1999). On the other hand, some members of Generation X and the millennial generation may appreciate living in large, free-standing single-family homes with yards that are located in neighborhoods with good schools and child-focused amenities such as playgrounds, sports facilities, and afternoon enrichment classes (Moos et al., 2018). As the baby boomer and millennial generations are fairly large, their demand for small units in walkable neighborhoods has driven up house prices and rents over the past few years, resulting in housing affordability challenges for many, and especially on the east and west coasts of the United States (Dougherty, 2021).

The *generational groups* have become increasingly racially and ethnically diverse over the past several decades. For example, the group of people born before 1960 (including the greatest generation, the silent generation, and a large portion of the baby boomer generation) were 75% non–Hispanic White, 10% Black/African American, 4.6% Asian, and 9.1% Hispanic/Latino in 2015 (Frey, 2018b; the most recent information as of this writing). By contrast, millennials were 55.8% non–Hispanic White, 13.9% Black/African American, 6.4% Asian, and 20.8% Hispanic/Latino in 2015 (Frey, 2018b; the most recent information as of this writing). This racial and ethnic diversity has been projected to increase in the future, resulting in the U.S. becoming majority minority in 2045, when 49.7% of the population will be non–Hispanic White, 13.1% will be Black/African American, 7.9% will be Asian, and 24.6% will be Hispanic/Latino (Frey, 2018c; the most recent information as of this writing).

The increase in racial and ethnic diversity can be attributed to several factors, including the increase in the proportion of the population that is foreign-born, the increase in the number and proportion of multiracial and multiethnic marriages, and the higher birth rates of women of color. The proportion of foreign-born people has steadily increased from 4.7% (or 9.6 million) in 1970, facilitated by the Immigration and Naturalization Act of 1965 that lifted restrictive national quotas, to 14.6% (or 47.9 million) in September 2022, just below record highs in 1890 and 1910 (Camarota & Zeigler, 2022). This proportion has been projected to reach 18% by 2065 (Frey, 2018d; Lopez & Passel, 2015; the most recent information as of this writing).

Similarly, the number and proportion of multiracial and multiethnic marriages have increased over the past few decades. For example, 3% of marriages were multiracial in 1967, while about 19% of marriages were multiracial or multiethnic in 2019 (Parker & Barroso, 2021). The largest proportion of multiracial and multiethnic marriages was between non-Hispanic Whites and Hispanics/Latinos (45%), followed by all other (20%), non-Hispanic Whites and Asians (16%), and non-Hispanic Whites and Blacks/African Americans (8%) in the 2011 to 2015 timeframe (Frey, 2018a; the most recent information as of this writing).

However, racial and ethnic groups have had *different birth rates* (i.e., the number of births per 1,000 women between ages 15 to 44; Centers for Disease Control and Prevention, n.d.e). While the overall birth rate was at a historic low of 11.4 in 2019, compared to 23.7 births in 1960, 18.4 in 1970, 15.9 in 1980, 16.7 in 1990, 14.4 in 2000, and 12.4 births in 2015, birth rates were higher for Hispanics/Latinos (14.6 births) and Blacks/African Americans (13.4 births), but lower for Asians (13.0 births) and non-Hispanic Whites (9.8 births) in 2019 (Centers for Disease Control and Prevention, n.d.e; the most recent information as of this writing). The number of births among non-Hispanic White females is below the replacement level (i.e., an insufficient number of births to replace the total non-Hispanic White population; Frey, 2018a).

The increase in racial and ethnic diversity may result in different housing demands by different groups. For example, the average household of Somali refugees in Minneapolis, Minnesota, is relatively large due to a high number of children and possibly relatives (e.g., 3.90 versus 2.25 in Minnesota in 2008 and 2000, respectively) and the average household income is relatively low due to the relatively low number of years spent in education, relatively high rates of unemployment, and the lack of a written language in Somalia until the early 1970s (Dischinger, 2009). Most Somali refugees prefer homes with many rooms, which allow them to separate residents and visitors by gender and by the formality versus informality of visits (Hadjiyanni, 2007). For example, they prefer having up to two children per bedroom in separate twin beds, at least two gender-separated formal living rooms that facilitate planned and impromptu visits, and at least one informal family room that facilitates children's play and studying (Hadjiyanni, 2007). As most Somali refugees are Muslim, they are not allowed to pay mortgage interest and thus cannot become homeowners through conventional lending (Hadjiyanni, 2007). In sum, many Somali refugees live in unaffordable, overcrowded rental units that do not allow them to live according to their cultural preferences (Xiong, 2017).

6

HOUSING AFFORDABILITY

Housing affordability is a *policy concern*, as households burdened with high housing expenditures may have fewer resources left to pay for food, utilities, health and child care expenditures, transportation to work, emergencies, retirement, and professional opportunities, such as pursuing higher education or starting a business (Anacker, 2019). Until recently, housing affordability had especially been a challenge in many communities along the east and west coasts and in metropolitan areas with competitive labor markets (Anacker, 2019).

Indeed, housing affordability worsened during the COVID-19 pandemic. Rents in most large, dense cities decreased in 2020 and early 2021 because many renters moved to smaller, less dense cities or remote areas, resulting in a large proportion of vacant units (Anacker, 2022). However, rents in many cities have increased again since late 2021, after COVID-19 vaccines became widely available and the economy gradually began to recover (Rodriguez, 2023). For example, the asking rents of professionally managed units increased 23.9% from March 2020 to March 2023 nationwide (Joint Center for Housing Studies of Harvard University, 2023).

On the *supply side*, recent reasons for increasing rents include housing providers and property managers passing on increased expenditures for (deferred) unit maintenance and improvements to buyers and renters, responding to increased housing demand and possibly trying to make up for lost rental revenues during the pandemic or trying to increase profit (de la Campa & Reina, 2023; DePillis, 2022). On the *demand side*, reasons for the increasing rents

DOI: 10.1201/9781032657646-7

include many (although not all) renters returning to large, dense cities they had left at the beginning of the pandemic, increasing household formation rates, and some renters living on their own instead of sharing housing in order to have more space for remote work and leisure activities from home (Thompson, 2022).

Nationwide, *nominal prices* (i.e., not adjusted for inflation) of existing homes increased 37.5%, translating into an increase of median sales prices from $283,000 to $375,400 from March 2020 to March 2023 (Joint Center for Housing Studies of Harvard University, 2023). On the *supply side*, one recent reason for increasing house prices has been increased construction labor costs due to worker shortages (many Hispanic/Latino workers returned to their countries of origin during the Great Recession and the pandemic and in periods when the federal government had an anti-immigrant stance), the decreasing interest in construction jobs, and higher wages. Another recent reason for increasing house prices is the vast increase in the cost of inputs in new residential construction, including plastic construction, gypsum, lumber, wood products, ready-mix concrete, and brick and clay structural tile (Joint Center for Housing Studies of Harvard University, 2023). Another reason is the increase in mortgage interest rates, as discussed in Chapter 4.

On the *demand side*, one recent reason for increasing house prices is an increased number and proportion of households, including the largest of all generational groups, the millennials, mentioned in Chapter 5. Some millennials may have postponed forming households because of the Great Recession and the delayed recovery, followed by the COVID-19 pandemic, as well as long-term concerns about student debt (Davidovich et al., 2021; Koch, 2019; Sternberg, 2019). Recently, the incomes of most households have increased nominally, while only some incomes may have increased in real terms (i.e., adjusted for the relatively high inflation rate) (Bremen, 2023). Many households compete in housing markets with very limited housing supply, although current, high mortgage interest rates may have put a damper on homebuying for some households (Goodman & Neal, 2022).

Housing affordability may be measured in several ways, including the *housing expenditure-to-income ratio*, the *housing wage*, and the *residual income approach* (Anacker & Li, 2016). First, the U.S. Department of Housing and Urban Development, among many other institutions, utilizes the *housing expenditure-to-income ratio*. Whenever a household has housing costs (i.e., rent or mortgage, insurance, and property tax payments, as well as any utility costs) higher than 30% of its gross income (before taxes), it is termed "cost burdened;" whenever a household has costs higher than 50%, it is termed "severely cost burdened" (Alvarez & Steffen, 2021; Bull & Gross, 2023; U.S. Department of Housing and Urban Development, 2017a, n.p.). The Center for Neighborhood Technology (CNT) suggests the Housing and Transportation (H+T®) Affordability Index which combines housing and transportation costs, setting the threshold of 45% of household income (Center for Neighborhood Technology, n.d.).

Over the past two decades or so, the number of cost-burdened renters has steadily increased, from 20.4 million in 2019 to 21.6 million (or 49% of all renters) in 2021, 11.6 million of which were severely cost burdened (Alvarez & Steffen, 2021; Joint Center for Housing Studies of Harvard University, 2023). Housing cost burdens disproportionately affect households with low incomes, including 86% with household incomes of less than $15,000, 68% with household incomes between $15,000 and $29,999, 63% with incomes between $30,000 and $44,999, and 34% with incomes between $45,000 and $74,999 (Alvarez & Steffen, 2021; Joint Center for Housing Studies of Harvard University, 2023). Between 2019 and 2021, the latter two groups had relatively large increases in their proportions of housing cost burdens (three and four percentage points, respectively; Alvarez & Steffen, 2021; Joint Center for Housing Studies of Harvard University, 2023).

Second, the National Low Income Housing Coalition (NLIHC) suggests the *housing wage*, based on the hourly wage a full-time worker needs to earn to rent a unit without paying more than 30% of their income on housing. In 2023, the national housing wage was $23.67 per hour for a modest one-bedroom unit and $28.58 per hour for a modest two-bedroom unit, both in decent condition (Aurand et al., 2023). By contrast, the federal minimum wage was $7.25 per hour, although 30 states, the District of Columbia, and Puerto Rico, as well as 66 counties and municipalities, had minimum wages that were higher than the federal minimum wage in 2023 (Aurand et al., 2023).

Thus, an average minimum-wage worker would need to work 86 hours per week (out of 168, or slightly more than two full-time jobs) to rent a one-bedroom and 104 hours per week (or about 2.6 full-time jobs) to rent a two-bedroom unit (Aurand et al., 2023). An average renter has an hourly wage of $23.68, one cent higher than the national one-bedroom housing wage ($23.67) but $4.90 less than the national two-bedroom housing wage ($28.58; Aurand et al., 2023). Indeed, 10 of the 20 most common occupations pay median wages that are below the one-bedroom housing wage, including food and beverage service workers ($14.27); retail sales workers ($14.88); cooks and food preparation workers ($15.35); home health and personal care aides, nursing assistants, orderlies, and psychiatric aides ($15.78); and building cleaning and pest control workers ($15.85) (Aurand et al., 2023).

Third, Stone (2006, 2009a, 2009b) suggests the *residual income approach*, which is the amount a household can still spend on housing after they have accounted for other necessary expenditures of living. His suggestion is based on the insight that housing costs are inflexible or fixed, as discussed above.

There are many ideas about *addressing housing affordability* while serving low- and moderate-income households ("Duty to Serve") (Ratcliffe et al., 2022). For example, the FHFA introduced two Equitable Housing Finance Plans (EHFPs) at the federal level in 2022. Fannie Mae's *Equitable Housing Finance Plan* is a three-year roadmap that first focused on Black/African American households in 2022, although its updated 2023 plan also included Hispanic/Latino households. The Plan's primary objectives are reducing rental and homeownership costs, eliminating barriers to insufficient credit, and supporting long-term housing success for underserved borrowers and renters (Fannie Mae, 2023). Freddie Mac's *Equitable Housing Finance Plan* includes all households of color and suggests purchasing, insuring, and securitizing mortgages from lenders originated under Special Purpose Credit Programs (SPCPs), based on the Equal Credit Opportunity Act (ECOA), passed in 1974 (Freddie Mac, 2022). SPCPs may entail benefits such as expanded eligibility for mortgages, reduced pricing, or down payment assistance (Freddie Mac, 2022). There are also many ideas about addressing housing affordability at the state and local levels.

SUMMARY OF PART I

- Housing and neighborhoods mean many things to many people.
- Households, housing units, and neighborhoods undergo change over time.
- Regional and local stakeholders may influence neighborhoods.
- Abraham Maslow's hierarchy of human needs encompasses five consecutive levels of need: two physical needs (physiological needs and security and safety needs) and three social needs (sense of belonging, self-esteem or ego needs, and self-actualization needs).
- Although there is no right to housing in the U.S., it is an aspirational ideal embedded in Article 25 of the Universal Declaration of Human Rights of the United Nations.
- Housing supply and building cycles are influenced by many factors, including the state of the economy, access to mortgages and mortgage interest rates, developer market assessments, zoning, community responses, housing policy, and housing demand.
- Housing demand is influenced by many factors, including the population and its life expectancy, household incomes, household sizes, family lifecycle stages and multigenerational households, access to mortgages, and housing policy.
- Housing affordability is a policy concern, as households burdened with high housing expenditures have fewer resources to pay for other items.

DOI: 10.1201/9781032657646-8

PART II

HOUSING POLICY IN THE UNITED STATES

Public policy, or a system of guidelines, laws, and programs issued by federal, state, and local governments, responds to *societal challenges and needs*, as well as *market failures* (Bull & Gross, 2023; Desmond, 2023). While conservative policymakers favor less government intervention, especially when it protects the market and major investors in that market, democratic policymakers favor more government intervention that favors people, including those with limited opportunities (Bull & Gross, 2023). Public policies may be grouped by typology into *distributive, constituent, regulative,* and *redistributive policies* (Lowi, 1972). In terms of housing policy, an example of a *distributive policy* is the mortgage interest deduction (MID), which allows those who own and reside in their main homes and who have mortgage debts of less than $750,000 to itemize qualified expenses, including their property taxes and mortgage interest payments (Internal Revenue Service, n.d.). Examples of *constituent policies* include the establishment of the U.S. Department of Housing and Urban Development (HUD) in 1965 (replacing the FHA, established in 1937) and the Consumer Financial Protection Bureau (CFPB) in 2010/2011 (Federal Register, 2019). An example of a *regulative policy* is President Kennedy's Executive Order #11063 of 1962, which prohibits the use of federal funds, including those by the FHA and the VA. The goal of this Order is to address racial discrimination in housing and residential racial segregation (Anonymous, 1995; Rothstein, 2017; Vale, 2000). Finally, an example of a *redistributive policy* is the LIHTC program, which benefits affordable housing investors by reducing their federal income tax

DOI: 10.1201/9781032657646-9

(Shanholtz, 2016). About three decades ago, Hartman (1992) discussed the LIHTC program, used by many developers who build low-income housing, arguing that it feeds sparrows (i.e., the renters) by feeding horses (i.e., the developers). In sum, public policy is important because it provides regulations and benefits that are in the interest of society.

THE IMPORTANCE OF HOUSING POLICY

In 2019, 5% of U.S. households received some type of housing assistance (Alvarez & Steffen, 2021). However, fewer than 1% of the U.S. housing stock has public housing (Bull & Gross, 2023). The *U.S. housing policy landscape*, which has some surprising aspects, has been *balkanized* into dozens of programs, demonstrations, and initiatives. Until 2017, homeownership policy was primarily supported by tax policy, while rentership policy is currently supported by tax expenditures, as well as direct subsidies. Housing policy assists not only individuals, including low-income people who may be in need and middle-income people who may not necessarily be in need, but also companies, including developers and housing providers. Typically, housing policy has been reactive rather than proactive, as witnessed during three watershed movements in policy history: the Great Depression in the 1930s, the Civil Rights movement in the 1960s, and the Great Recession in the 2000s (Anacker, 2018). Interestingly, many programs that had been established during the Great Depression were used during the Great Recession in the late 2000s, although some argue that the federal response to the foreclosure crisis was "too little, too late, and too timid" (Immergluck, 2013).

Housing programs are not only administered at the federal, state, and local levels, they also have different administrative homes (Schwartz, 2021). For example, federal programs may be administered by several departments and agencies, including:

- the U.S. Department of Housing and Urban Development (HUD, which houses the Federal Housing Administration (FHA) and Ginnie Mae) (Schwartz, 2021);

DOI: 10.1201/9781032657646-10

- the Federal Housing Finance Agency (FHFA, which supervises the Federal Home Loan Bank (FHLB) system, Fannie Mae, and Freddie Mac) (Schwartz, 2021);
- the U.S. Department of Veterans Affairs (VA, which administers the VA Loan Guaranty Program to veterans (U.S. Department of Veterans Affairs, n.d.);
- the U.S. Department of the Treasury (which supervises the Internal Revenue Service (IRS) that in turn administers the Mortgage Interest Deduction (MID) (Internal Revenue Service, n.d.);
- the Consumer Financial Protection Bureau (which provides consumer education on many financial aspects, including saving for down payment, student loans, and mortgages) (Kirsch & Squires, 2017); and
- the U.S. Department of Agriculture (USDA, which administers rural housing programs; not discussed due to space constraint) (U.S. Department of Agriculture, n.d.a).

This split in departments and agencies may also occur at state and local levels. *Housing programs* may be implemented by public, private, or nonprofit institutions. For example, the federal government may implement a program itself; it may delegate program implementation to a state government, as in the case of the LIHTC program, or to a local government, as in the case of the CDBG program; or it may delegate program implementation to a for-profit or nonprofit institution (Schwartz, 2021).

Over time, there has been a *devolution* from the federal to state governments and then from state to local governments, starting in 1973, when President Nixon declared a moratorium on federal housing and community development assistance, including funding for public housing (Bull & Gross, 2023; Hays, 2012). Also, there has been a shift from programs that invest in constructing, rehabilitating, renovating, and maintaining public housing stock (as in the case of public housing) to programs that invest in public–private partnerships (as in the case of the Homeownership Opportunities for People Everywhere (HOPE) VI public housing redevelopment program) or depend on the private housing stock (as in the case of housing choice vouchers) (Bratt, 2020).

URBAN HOUSING POLICY AND OWNER-OCCUPIED HOUSING AND THE GREAT DEPRESSION, THE CIVIL RIGHTS ERA, AND THE GREAT RECESSION

8.1 HOUSING POLICY AND THE GREAT DEPRESSION

During the Great Depression of the 1930s, Congress established several policies and programs to address the national foreclosure, lending, economic, and unemployment crises by assisting borrowers in default, establishing a new lending infrastructure with an innovative mortgage product (i.e., the amortizing 30-year mortgage with a fixed interest rate), and stimulating housing construction overall (U.S. Department of Housing and Urban Development, n.d.g).

Homeownership has been facilitated by housing policy for more than eight decades, including the MID (Schwartz, 2021). In 1929, the stock market crash worsened the Great Depression, which impacted many employees and businesses through a rapid decrease in household incomes, consumer demand, and business credit, resulting in a slower business volume, unemployment, business closures, and a large decrease in housing construction (Watkins, 1993). The Great Depression also affected banks through savers' and shareholders' fear of bank failures, which resulted in bank runs to withdraw savings, recalled loans, further decreasing bank reserves, and eventually insolvencies and further bank failures due to possible contagion effects (Benson, 2007; Gruenberg, 2023). Furthermore, the Great Depression also resulted in evictions, a nationwide foreclosures rate of 10–20%, and thousands of cases of

DOI: 10.1201/9781032657646-11

forbearance (Fishback et al., 2013; Metzger, 1998). Finally, the Great Depression impacted building and loan societies (B&Ls) and savings and loan societies (S&Ls), the primary providers of residential mortgage financing for single-family homes in the early 1930s, when many borrowers defaulted and then foreclosed on their homes, causing many B&Ls and S&Ls to go bankrupt (Mason, 2004).

In the early 1930s, the government's *New Deal* program introduced many national public and semipublic institutions, policies, and programs; except for the Home Owners' Loan Corporation (HOLC), all of these institutions, policies, and programs have continued operating and have facilitated homeownership for many borrowers until today (Highsmith, 2015). As a response to the Great Depression from a broad consensus that demanded government action, U.S. Congress established several policies and programs to address the national foreclosure, lending, economic, and unemployment crises by assisting borrowers in default, establishing a new lending infrastructure with an innovative mortgage product, and stimulating housing construction overall (U.S. Department of Housing and Urban Development, n.d.g). Examples of public and semipublic institutions, policies, and programs established through these policies include the *Federal Home Loan Bank (FHLB)* system in 1932, the *Home Owners' Loan Corporation (HOLC)* in 1933, the *Federal Deposit Insurance Corporation (FDIC)* in 1933, the *FHA* in 1934, and *Fannie Mae* in 1938 (Manturuk et al., 2017).

One direct, immediate, and long-term outcome of these public and semipublic institutions, policies, and programs has been a huge drop in bank runs and recalled loans, which were quite common before the 1930s, often followed by a recession (Bernanke, 2022; Hetzel, 2012; Leonard, 2022; Roberts, 2012). For example, there were about 600 failed banks per year from 1921 to 1929, 1,350 failed banks in 1930, and 2,203 failed banks in 1931 (Cromie et al., 2017; Federal Deposit Insurance Corporation, n.d.a., n.d.b; Shibut, 2017). In contrast, there were more than 600 failed banks between 1980 and 1994 and 489 insolvent and failed banks from 2008 to 2013, the vast majority of which were acquired by solvent banks, with the exception of Penn Square, which went bankrupt in 1982, and Lehman Brothers Holding, Inc., which filed for Chapter 11 bankruptcy in 2008 (Cromie et al., 2017; Federal Deposit Insurance Corporation, n.d.a, n.d.b; Leonard, 2022; Shibut, 2017).

Another indirect and long-term outcome of public and semipublic institutions, policies, and programs has been the increased and accelerated national homeownership rate (Dietz & Haurin, 2003; U.S. Bureau of the Census, n.d.c). In the pre-Depression era (i.e., from 1890 to 1930), the national homeownership rate hovered around 46.5%, plus or minus 1.5%; during the so-called transition era (i.e., from 1940 to 1970), it increased from 43.6% to about 65%; and in the so-called modern era (i.e., after 1970), the rate hovered around 65%, plus or minus 2%, although it temporarily peaked at 69% in 2004, during the house price bubble (Layton, 2021).

The financial landscape of more than a century ago was very different from today's landscape. In the late 19th and early 20th centuries, residential mortgage lenders were primarily either building and loan societies (B&Ls) or savings and loan associations (S&Ls) (Bodfish, 1931). Banks primarily made commercial loans and only gradually started originating residential mortgages after 1900, but they did not offer savings accounts (Bodfish, 1931). Life insurance companies primarily originated mortgages to businesses in cities throughout the nation and to farms primarily in the western part of the United States (Snowden, 2003). Thus, many prospective homebuyers saved their cash that they stockpiled at home, informally arranged loans through relatives or friends, or obtained mortgages with individual lenders, some of whom might be considered loan sharks (Weiss, 2002).

B&Ls were established in the United States from the 1830s until the 1950s, modeled after a building society established in Birmingham, England, in 1781 (Piquet, 1930; Wright, 1894). The early B&Ls benefitted from the movement to cities and the westward migration, as many city dwellers had factory jobs with regular, albeit small, wages, enabling them to save for homeownership (Riegel & Doubman, 1927). The number of B&Ls remained very small in their first five decades, partly due to the Civil War that raged from 1861 to 1865, but then increased in the 1880s during a period of rapid urbanization, with increased home building activity facilitated by mortgage lending (Teck, 1968). B&Ls were local cooperatives with typically less than 200 members that were initially self-regulated, possibly based on bylaws. After the 1880s, they were typically organized under general incorporation laws, and they were supervised by state agencies, state commissioners of banking or insurance, or by the state auditor himself after the 1920s (Riegel & Doubman, 1927). In other words, B&Ls were typically not state-chartered.

B&Ls were based on the share accumulation plan, in which each non-borrowing member, after having in some cases paid an entrance fee, pledged to buy shares in the association by paying regular weekly or monthly dues until his or her investment reached a predetermined maturity value (Dexter, 1889). Then, once a certain amount was reached, a non-borrowing member became a borrowing member who could take out a mortgage based on a mortgage contract (Bodfish, 1931; Dexter, 1889). Non-borrowers and borrowers fully shared the risks and rewards of the association's mortgage portfolio (Snowden, 1997, 2003). Unlike bank customers, B&L members were the legal owners of the thrift and thus could not demand immediate withdrawal of deposits, preventing bank runs (Mason, 2004). Members aimed for relatively high dividends of their shares but low interest rates on their mortgages, while at the same time trying to keep administrative expenses to a minimum (Dexter, 1889).

In the 1930s and 1940s, the local and regional B&L movement gradually morphed into the regional and national S&L (sometimes called "thrifts") industry, as the federal S&L charter, the Federal Home Loan Bank (FHLB), the Federal Deposit Insurance Corporation (FDIC), and many other associated regulations were established that enabled S&Ls to gradually expand to the national level (Anacker, 2015a). Most S&Ls primarily served small savers and borrowers, unlike many banks (Marvell, 1969). Interestingly, the federal government only allowed S&Ls to pay interest rates on deposits that were substantially below the interest rates on deposits paid by banks and also limited their ability to originate mortgages (Hays, 2012). Most S&Ls funded the long-term, fixed-rate mortgages that they often held in their portfolios with short-term deposits ("borrowing short to lend long") (Bernanke, 2022). This strategy became increasingly risky in the late 1970s and early 1980s, when inflation and interest rates dramatically increased, causing a funding crunch for most S&Ls (Robinson, 2013). Although regulators responded by deregulating the S&L industry and allowed paying higher interest rates on deposits in the early 1980s, a vast number of S&Ls collapsed, were bailed out by taxpayers, and were absorbed by banks in the late 1980s and 1990s (Bernanke, 2022; Mason, 2004).

An additional response from Congress to the Great Depression, the nationwide foreclosure crisis, and the dearth of lending was the

Federal Home Loan Bank Act in 1932. This Act established the Reconstruction Finance Corporation (RFC), an independent agency of the federal government that provided loans to or bought ownership stakes of several hundred lenders; assisted manufacturing and railroad companies; and then supported state relief programs for public works programs from 1932 to 1957 (Bloom, 2008; Fishback et al., 2013). It also established the *Federal Home Loan Bank (FHLB)* system, a "low visibility agency" that seldom deals directly with the public (Marvell, 1969, p. 3). The FHLB system is a financial services corporation funded by fees generated by FHLB loans (Thomson & Koepke, 2010). However, the FHLB system is a GSE with the implicit backing of the federal government (i.e., the U.S. Department of the Treasury) (Thomson & Koepke, 2010). The Federal Home Loan Bank Board (the Federal Housing Finance Board (FHFB) from 1989 to 2008 and the Federal Housing Finance Agency (FHFA) since 2008) originally supervised 12 (11 since 2015) regional Federal Home Loan Banks, which in turn supervise banking member institutions (Bernanke, 2022; Marvell, 1969). The members own equity stakes, also called shares, in their FHLBs in their respective districts of the FHLB system (Gissler & Narajabad, 2017a).

The FHLB system has three goals. First, it provides *secondary liquidity to mortgage lending institutions* that have temporary cash flow problems (Fishback et al., 2013). Second, it *transfers loanable funds* from surplus to saving deficit areas. Third, it attempts to *stabilize the residential construction and financing industries* (Keating, 1998). In the past, lenders held most mortgages in their portfolios until they were paid off. Securitization through the secondary mortgage market allowed lenders to sell their mortgages to Wall Street in exchange for upfront cash, moving mortgages off their books and enabling them to originate additional mortgages that they could sell for securitization (Engel & McCoy, 2011). The FHLB system, Fannie Mae, and Freddie Mac have all taken advantage of the secondary mortgage market, thus providing finances to fuel the post-World War II (suburban) housing boom (Schwartz, 2021).

In 1933, Congress established the *Home Owners' Loan Corporation (HOLC)*, a public agency under the Federal Home Loan Bank System, to respond to the large increase in unemployment that resulted in a dearth of business in the construction industry and a large number and proportion of mortgage defaults and home foreclosures that ultimately led to a decrease in the homeownership rate and national house prices of around 35% (Fishback et al., 2013; Freund, 2007). At the beginning, HOLC had $200 million (interest-free) in Treasury funds at its disposal and the authority to issue bonds of up to $2 billion to finance operations for its first three years (Fishback et al., 2013; Freund, 2007). Later, HOLC sent $3.1 billion in early 1934 and then $4.75 billion in May 1935 to regional federal banks to refinance homes until 1936 (Baxandall & Ewen, 2000; Fishback et al., 2013). While the federal government guaranteed only the interest until April 1934, it began guaranteeing both interest and the principal of the bonds after April 1934 (Fishback et al., 2013). The Corporation assisted struggling financial institutions by purchasing defaulting ("toxic") mortgages for pennies on the dollar, assisting struggling eligible borrowers of properties with a value up to $20,000 by refinancing mortgages for up to 80% of the appraised value of the home, followed by restructuring and servicing the mortgages (Fishback et al., 2013; Glantz, 2019). During its first 18 months or so, HOLC established more than 400 offices with about 20,000 staff nationwide (Fishback et al., 2013).

The delinquent mortgages refinanced and reissued under HOLC had several innovative housing finance components (Baxandall & Ewen, 2000):

- They were *fully amortized* (i.e., mortgages were paid off at the end of their lifecycle).
- They had a relatively *high loan-to-value (LTV) ratio* of 80% and a relatively *low maximum interest rate* of 5% (reduced to 4.5% in 1939; compared to 6–8% in the private sector).
- They had *longer durations* of up to 15 years, which was expanded to 20 and then 25 years in 1939.
- They had an optional three-year period when only mortgage interest (not principal) payments could be made until June 1936 (Fishback et al., 2013; Rothstein, 2017).

The latter three components resulted in lower monthly payments during the life of the loan (Baxandall & Ewen, 2000). HOLC also provided cash advances to borrowers to pay taxes and make necessary home repairs (Crossney & Bartelt, 2005; Fishback et al., 2013). By 1936, when HOLC stopped providing mortgages, it had received 1.9 million applications from June 1933 to June 1935 and had refinanced about 1 million mortgages with a total of $3.1 billion (Metzger, 1998). Keating (1998) states that HOLC had refinanced about 1.8 million mortgages by the time it was liquidated in 1954.

HOLC's overall rejection rate was 46% (Fishback et al., 2013). Rejection reasons were inadequate security (17.9% of all rejected, incomplete, or withdrawn applications); a lack of distress (12.6%); an applicant failing to cooperate (9.7%); an ineligible property (i.e., not a homestead; 8.0%); a lender's refusal to accept bonds (7.7%); a borrower having unstable credit or income (7.5%); an ineligible property (i.e., primarily commercial use; 4.8%); and a defective or insufficient title (3.5%) (Fishback et al., 2013). Also, there were miscellaneous rejection reasons (12.7%) and withdrawn applications (15.6%) (Fishback et al., 2013).

While most scholars state that HOLC refinanced about one million mortgages by 1936, there seems to be some debate about the proportion of properties it assisted. Colton (2003) reports that HOLC assisted about 40% of 4.8 million properties, or one in four units (about 1.92 million), and that it refinanced about 20% of all outstanding non-farm mortgages of owner-occupied properties, based on Doan (1997; see also Fishback et al., 2013). However, Baxandall and Ewen (2000), Fishback et al. (2013), and Metzger (1998) state that HOLC assisted about 10% of the non-farm housing stock, and Glantz (2019, p. 23) states that HOLC helped refinance "one in five mortgages in urban America." Colton (2003), based on the U.S. Bureau of the Census (1975), stated that at the peak of HOLC's activity in 1935, it held 12% of the entire outstanding national residential mortgage debt, a higher proportion than either life insurance companies or commercial banks held in their portfolios. However, only 5% of HOLC's refinanced mortgages had been held by Black/African American borrowers (Freund, 2007). Despite all these efforts, about 20% of borrowers who refinanced their mortgages with HOLC defaulted (Fishback et al., 2013). The average loss of each foreclosure was about 30% (Fishback et al., 2013).

In sum, "the incredible HOLC," the largest single residential mortgage lender in the mid-1930s, may be seen as a success due to the large number and proportion of businesses and borrowers assisted and because it was an innovative mortgage product that was later modified by the FHA (Crossney & Bartelt, 2005; Fishback et al.,

2013). Others point out that while HOLC's activities led to increased house prices and homeownership rates, it did not "completely reverse the damage" (Fishback et al., 2013, p. x). Some argue that HOLC may have prevented the collapse of the entire mortgage industry (Baxandall & Ewen, 2000); others emphasize that HOLC made a small profit (Crossney & Bartelt, 2005); and still others argue that it lost about $53 million, or about 2% of its total lending volume of around $3 billion, concluding that "HOLC was not free, but neither did it cost taxpayers much money in the grand scheme of the federal budget" (Fishback et al., 2013, p. 8).

The *National Industrial Recovery Act*, passed in 1933, enabled the *Public Works Administration (PWA)*, a temporary federal public works construction agency that funded jobs in construction and provided housing from 1935 to 1944 (The Living New Deal, n.d.). The PWA acted as a developer itself or provided loans and grants to cover up to 30% of a project's costs for state or municipal agencies, which in turn selected projects and then hired private contractors or limited-dividend corporations (The Living New Deal, n.d.). Between 1933 and 1937, the PWA was awarded $3.8 billion and constructed 34,000 projects, including large-scale projects such as highways, streets, bridges, dams, schools, and hospitals, among others (Rothstein, 2017).

The *Banking Act of 1933* enabled the establishment of the *Federal Deposit Insurance Corporation (FDIC)*, a government corporation, after several banks failed during the Great Depression (Anonymous, n.d.). The FDIC charters banks and examines approximately 5,850 institutions, about 2,250 of which are members of the Federal Reserve System and about 3,600 of which are nonmembers but are state-chartered (Anonymous, n.d.; Law, 2018). The FDIC provides deposit insurance to U.S. commercial banks and savings institutions through its Deposit Insurance Fund, funded by the dues of members and the interest on the investment of these deposited dues, as determined by the institution's level of capitalization and its potential risk (Anonymous, n.d.). As of this writing, the FDIC insures about $13 trillion of deposits (Anonymous, n.d.).

Furthermore, the FDIC examines institutions for safety and soundness to comply with consumer laws, such as the Fair Housing Act of 1968, the Truth in Lending Act (TILA) of 1968, the Real Estate Settlement Procedures Act (RESPA) of 1974, the Equal Credit Opportunity Act (ECOA) of 1974, the Home Mortgage

Disclosure Act of 1975 (HMDA), the Community Reinvestment Act of 1977 (CRA), and the Home Ownership and Equity Protection Act (HOEPA) of 1994 (Anonymous, n.d.; Hashimzade et al., 2017). Moreover, the FDIC approves or disapproves institutional mergers, consolidations, acquisitions, requests for establishing new or closing existing branches, and requests for moving main offices (Anonymous, n.d.). Finally, it maintains a list of failed banks and provides information on how accounts are affected (Anonymous, n.d.).

The *Federal Housing Administration (FHA)* is a government agency that was enabled by the National Housing Act of 1934 "to meet President Roosevelt's desire for at least one program that could stimulate building without government spending and that would rely instead on private enterprise" (Jackson, 1985, p. 203). The FHA, housed under the U.S. Department of Housing and Urban Development since it was established in 1965, insures mortgages made by FHA-approved lenders but does not originate mortgages (Erickson, 2009). In case the borrower defaults on the mortgage, the FHA pays the lender (not the borrower), possesses the home, and repays the lender the remaining amount owed (Jones, 2019; Schwartz, 2019). Many other FHA innovations and business practices have served as the basis for other public programs and private housing finance products (Freeman, 2019). Since its inception in 1934, the FHA has insured more than 46 million mortgages (U.S. Department of Housing and Urban Development, n.d.g). By 1950, the FHA and the Veterans Administration (VA) together had insured half of all new mortgages (Rothstein, 2017). According to Jackson (1985, p. 203), "[n]o agency of the United States government has had a more pervasive and powerful impact on the American people over the past half-century than the Federal Housing Administration (FHA)."

Prior to the establishment of the FHA in 1934, down payment requirements were often more than 50%, repayment schedules were short (typically five years), and balloon payments at the end of loan terms were large (Schwartz, 2021). The FHA designed the 20- to 30-year, standardized, low down payment, low-interest, fixed-rate, amortizing mortgage for single-family homes in its popular Section 203(b) program (Austen, 2018). As of this writing, Section 203(b) FHA-insured mortgages require a relatively low down payment of 3.5% from the borrower (U.S. Department of Housing and Urban

Development, n.d.g). According to Hays (2012, p. 89), "the working- or middle-class family with modest but steady incomes now found mortgage payments within reach."

Typical borrowers of FHA-insured mortgages are first-time homebuyers who have relatively low household incomes, are young, and are disproportionately Black/African American or Hispanic/Latino (Golding et al., 2014; Immergluck, 2011; U.S. Department of Housing and Urban Development, 2022). For example, 83.52% of FHA-insured mortgages were made to first-time borrowers in 2021, compared to 46.50% of the remainder of the market (U.S. Department of Housing and Urban Development, 2022). About 43.75% of FHA-insured mortgages were taken out by low-income borrowers (i.e., households with incomes below 80% of the area median income (AMI)) in 2021, relative to 22.91% of any other mortgage (U.S. Department of Housing and Urban Development, 2022). While 44.25% of FHA-insured mortgages were originated to borrowers under the age of 35 in 2021, only 37.63% of VA-insured mortgages and 32.93% of conventional mortgages were (U.S. Department of Housing and Urban Development, 2022).

While the FHA has served many first-time, young, low-income, non-Hispanic White homebuyers relatively well over the past eight decades, it has only recently begun serving some first-time, young, low-income homebuyers of color. For example, in 2021, 60.21% and 61.30% of mortgages with an LTV ratio higher than 95% went to Black/African American and Hispanic/Latino borrowers, respectively (U.S. Department of Housing and Urban Development, 2022).

From 1934 to the early to mid-1960s, the FHA almost exclusively benefitted non-Hispanic White borrowers who bought new, single-family, detached homes in non-Hispanic White suburbs that were predicted to retain their current racial and socioeconomic composition (Vale, 2000). While disproportionately benefitting non-Hispanic White borrowers, the FHA denied homeownership opportunities to the vast majority of Blacks/African Americans and Hispanics/Latinos, who, on the basis of their race and ethnicity, were not eligible for FHA-insured loans and thus continued renting in cities, possibly making them unable to build intergenerational wealth through homeownership (Coates, 2017). Indeed, from 1946 to 1959, only 2% of new homes insured by the FHA were occupied by Blacks/African Americans (Black & Robinson, 1959).

FHA's practices were based on historic mortgage underwriting ratios and the risk-rating system adopted from the HOLC, which had previously adopted them from the real estate industry based on biased attitudes and predictions about the trajectory of property values, based on the race and ethnicity of community residents (Federal Housing Administration, 1939). FHA's risk-rating system was based on a household's mortgage risk and the predicted neighborhood stability based on its racial and ethnic composition (Rothstein, 2017).

The FHA initially enforced racially biased restrictive covenants (i.e., legal instruments included in a property's deed that enabled non-Hispanic White owners to preclude the sale of homes to Blacks/African Americans and other races or ethnicities) (Dreier et al., 2014). The FHA thus "redlined the cities, speeding the migration of the white middle class out of the older central cities," which contributed to residential racial and ethnic *de facto* and *de jure* segregation (Dreier et al., 2014, p. 121). While *de facto* segregation has been caused by individual prejudices, household income and wealth differences, and the decisions made by real estate agents and lenders, *de jure* segregation has been caused by laws, policies, and programs passed by federal, state, and local governments (Rothstein, 2017). Indeed, according to Rothstein (2017, p. 70), "[t]he FHA had its biggest impact on segregation, not in its discriminatory evaluations of individual mortgage applicants, but in its financing of entire subdivisions, in many cases entire suburbs, as racially exclusive white enclaves."

Redlining is the systematic denial of services, including originating mortgages, and discrimination on the basis of race, color, religion, national origin, gender, disability, and the presence of children in the household, all of which created racial ghettos for many years (Popkin, 2018). Although the U.S. Supreme Court ruled in 1948 in *Shelly v. Kraemer* that state courts were prohibited from enforcing racially biased restrictive covenants, triggered by a lawsuit advanced by the NAACP, and although the FHA revised its underwriting manual in 1950 to factor in *Shelly v. Kraemer*, the FHA nevertheless continued to favor racial discrimination and segregation and to refrain from challenging racial and ethnic steering and redlining (Rothstein, 2017). In the mid-1950s, the FHA began to soften its exclusionary stance and gradually made substantial investments toward expanding FHA insurance to Blacks/African Americans (Wiese, 2004).

8.2 HOUSING POLICY AND THE CIVIL RIGHTS ERA

From the early to mid-1960s to the beginning of the Great Recession, the FHA gradually expanded its activities to include borrowers of color and challenged neighborhoods, including through Section 223(e) after 1968 (Hays, 2012). However, much of the FHA's lending to Blacks/African Americans was marred by reckless, fraudulent, discriminatory, predatory, and unsustainable financial practices. Starting in the 1960s,

> [l]enders found that they could join local real estate agents in exploiting racial fears and fomenting racial change in order to create a huge volume of sales in certain areas. *Their motivation was to make as many loans as possible to minorities, not to exclude them.* In fact, the financial incentives were so great that scores of real estate agents, lenders, and even FHA officials engaged in fraud, in order to make sales to unqualified and unsuspecting minority homebuyers.
> (Bradford & Shlay, 1996, p. 80, italics in original)

While the national homeownership rate increased in the 1950s and 1960s, many *alternative home buying practices* became common for those excluded from the conventional homeownership market, including *land-installment practices* and *double sales schemes*. In *land-installment practices*, a speculator purchased a house and then added costly purchase and sales commissions, various financing charges, and overhead costs (Satter, 2009). Next, the speculator made largely cosmetic renovations to the property, also at a large profit margin, and then sold the house for an inflated price that was often as high as double the investor's purchase price (Satter, 2009). Before the purchase, the speculator took out two loans, one for the amount of the appraised value of the property and another for the difference between the appraised value and the sale price (Satter, 2009). These two loans were then packaged for the buyer, with the speculator retaining the title to the property but permitting the buyer immediate possession of the property until the second loan that covered the difference between the appraised value and the sale price was paid off (Satter, 2009). Then, a new conventional mortgage at the appraised value was taken out, at which time the purchaser retained the title to the property.

In *double sales schemes*, a property passed through the hands of two or more speculator-investors, increasing in price between transactions and finally being sold through Section 221(d)(2), FHA's low income/no down payment program, introduced in 1968 (Chatterjee et al., 1974). The impact of all of these layered fees and inflated prices was that buyers were effectively in negative equity at the time of purchase, thereby limiting if not precluding them from ever building any equity from their home purchases. Interestingly, FHA administrators and professionals in the housing industry were fully aware of these types of discriminatory transactions but took little if any action to eliminate them from the market.

In the 1960s and 1970s, Congress addressed racial and ethnic housing and credit discrimination, outlawed racially biased restrictive covenants and redlining, and required data reporting and deposit-taking lenders to reinvest in their communities through several orders and acts. First, President Kennedy's *Executive Order #11063* of 1962, which prohibits the use of federal funds, including those by the FHA and the VA. The goal of this Order is to address racial discrimination in housing and residential racial segregation (Anonymous, 1995).

Second, the *Fair Housing Act of 1968*, subsequently amended in 1988, not only invalidated racially biased restrictive covenants in 1968, it also prohibits housing discrimination by housing providers, realtors, and buyers and sellers of real estate on the basis of race, color, religion, national origin, gender, disability, the presence of children, sex, familial status, and disability, which are collectively known as "protected classes" (Howell, 2018; Squires, 2018). While the Fair Housing Act of 1968 prohibits discrimination, it did not reverse residential racial and ethnic segregation (Rothstein, 2017).

Third, the *Equal Credit Opportunity Act (ECOA) of 1974* prohibits credit discrimination based on race, color, religion, national origin, sex, marital status, age, or public assistance receipt (Federal Trade Commission, n.d.). While lenders may request this information from borrowers, they may not utilize it in loan decisions (Federal Trade Commission, n.d.). Instead, lenders base their lending decision on the borrower's creditworthiness (i.e., credit report information from the three major credit bureaus), income and employment history, and collaterals, such as home and car values, among others (Fair Isaac Corporation, n.d.a, n.d.b). The borrower's creditworthiness influences their ability to secure a lease for an apartment, utilize a credit card in case of a financial shock, and obtain a home or business loan, while also influencing the credit terms (Ratcliffe & Brown, 2017).

Fourth, the *Home Mortgage Disclosure Act (HMDA) of 1975* requires many but not all lenders to report lending data, including the date of the application and the mortgage origination; the purpose of the loan (i.e., purchase, refinance, or home improvement); the type, location, occupancy, and lien status of the property; the gender, race, and ethnicity of the mortgage applicant; and the outcome (i.e., originated, denied, withdrawn by applicant) of the application (Bhutta & Ringo, 2016). In 2022, 4,460 U.S. financial institutions reported their originated mortgage loans to HMDA, a number that excludes depository financial institutions that fall under a certain asset-size threshold, do not have a home or branch office located in a metropolitan statistical area, do not originate a single mortgage during the previous year, fail a federally related test, and fall under a certain loan–volume threshold (Consumer Financial Protection Bureau, 2023; Federal Financial Institutions Examination Council, 2019).

Non-depository financial institutions that do not have a home or branch office located in a metropolitan statistical area and fall under a certain asset-size threshold also do not report their originated mortgage loans (Federal Financial Institutions Examination Council, 2019). These institutions do not accept deposits but obtain funding from other banks (Taylor, 2019). An example of a non-depository financial institution is an independent mortgage bank (IMB), which was part of the mortgage lending boom in the early 2000s, when mortgage interest rates decreased and demand for homeownership increased, leading to increased house prices (Anacker & Crossney, 2013). Some argue that the rapid increase in the number of IMBs and the growth in their mortgage volumes at least correlated with, if not partially caused, the increase in subprime lending and subsequent foreclosures (Anacker & Crossney, 2013). IMBs originated about 60% of *all* mortgages and about 75% of those mortgages insured by Fannie Mae, Freddie Mac, and the FHA in 2022 (Goodman et al., 2023). IMB lending to low- and moderate-income neighborhoods with a high proportion of borrowers of color was much higher than bank lending, partly because first-time homebuyers, who have relatively low household incomes, are young, and are primarily Black/African American or Hispanic/Latino, disproportionately take out mortgages (Goodman et al., 2023).

Finally, the *Community Reinvestment Act (CRA) of 1977*, adopted as a reaction to redlining, allows federal regulators to sanction those lenders that accept local deposits but do not adequately serve their communities (Anacker & Crossney, 2013). However, the implementation and enforcement of these laws have been mediocre, partly due to inadequate enforcement provisions in those laws and partly due to insufficient funding. While these laws have reduced racial, ethnic, and economic discrimination, they have not eliminated it (Reid, 2020). Rather, housing discrimination shifted from open to covert discrimination, which is subtle and more difficult to challenge (Turner et al., 2013).

In addition to the FHLB system, the HOLC, the FDIC, and the *FHA*, U.S. Congress established *Fannie Mae*, a government-sponsored enterprise (GSE), in 1938. Fannie Mae purchases, insures, and bundles mortgages from lenders and then sells mortgage-backed securities (MBSs, e.g., bonds or securitized claims) to investors on Wall Street with guarantees of interest and principal, absorbing risk, expanding the so-called secondary mortgage market, and freeing up capital for additional mortgages (Johnson, J. A., 1996; Johnson & Kwak, 2010). Fannie Mae exemplifies the indirect homeownership support of the federal government, in addition to direct support through the MID.

The federal government tasked Fannie Mae with supporting homeownership by lowering the cost of mortgage credit for borrowers, later formalized through the affordable housing goals specified in the Federal Housing Enterprise Safety and Soundness Act of 1992 (Engel & McCoy, 2011). In return, Fannie Mae was granted several advantages that may be seen as preferential or special treatment, unfair competition, subsidies, or simply assistance fulfilling their charters, depending on one's point of view (Calabria, 2011; Reiss, 2011). Some of these advantages were the implicit federal guarantee of the payment of principal and interest on their MBSs, exemption from state and local taxes, and relatively low minimum capital requirements, among many others (Baily, 2011; Dynan & Gayer, 2011; Pozen, 2011; Zandi, 2009).

In the mid-1960s, while interest rates were increasing and housing construction and lending volume were thus decreasing, U.S. Congress became concerned about Fannie Mae's increased debt and the possibility of it becoming a potential government liability

(Hagerty, 2012; Wallison, 2011). Thus, Congress split Fannie Mae into two units in 1968: the Government National Mortgage Association (Ginnie Mae), which remained a government entity that guarantees mortgages insured by the FHA, the Veterans Administration, and the U.S. Department of Agriculture (Manturuk et al., 2017). Ginnie Mae also buys government-issued loans for high-risk, low-income housing programs at a higher rate and then sells them to investors on Wall Street at market rate, subsidizing the difference (Barth, 2009). Congress then privatized Fannie Mae, from then on owned by stockholders, although its public mission continued (Brandlee, 2011; Congressional Budget Office, 1991).

Originally, Fannie Mae had only been allowed to purchase mortgages insured by the FHA and the Veterans Administration, although they were also allowed to purchase conventional mortgages after 1970. In 1970, Congress established Freddie Mac to purchase, insure, and bundle mortgages originated by savings and loans and, later, by many lenders (Manturuk et al., 2017). Like Fannie Mae, Freddie Mac could then sell them to investors on Wall Street, issuing bonds or securitized claims, such as the MBS, absorbing risk and thus expanding the secondary mortgage market (Colton, 2003). Like Fannie Mae, Freddie Mac was also tasked with lowering the cost of mortgage credit, receiving preferential or special treatment from the government in return (Anacker, 2015a).

In addition to the public and semipublic institutions, policies, and programs established during the Great Depression, the U.S. passed the *Servicemen's Readjustment Act of 1944* (also called the *GI Bill*), which enabled the Veteran's Administration (VA) Loan Guaranty program that facilitated homeownership after World War II by insuring mortgages of veterans at a down payment of 0% (Baxandall & Ewen, 2000). However, the vast majority of Black/African American and other minority veterans were initially excluded from this benefit, most not even applying to the VA Loan Guaranty program, as they knew that the VA would reject them due to their race and ethnicity. For example, in New York and northern New Jersey, fewer than 100 of the 67,000 mortgages insured by the VA Loan Guaranty program were held by Blacks/African Americans (Katznelson, 2005).

The public and semipublic institutions, policies, and programs established in the 1930s as a response to the Great Depression addressed the national foreclosure, lending, economic, and unemployment crises by assisting borrowers in default and addressing the dearth of lending with a new lending infrastructure and an innovative mortgage product. However, construction of new homes was scant with the exception of the FHA, which built homes for workers in war-related industries (Talen, 2019). Similarly, rehabilitation and renovation of existing homes were scarce, resulting in buildings not being repaired or maintained well or at all, thus falling into substandard conditions (Colton, 2003). In sum, most inner cities had a housing stock that was aging, substandard, or even uninhabitable in the 1930s (Hays, 2012).

However, demand for housing has increased greatly since the end of World War II (Von Hoffman, 2003). Until the 1920s, hundreds of thousands of immigrants had moved to the U.S., often to inner cities in large metropolitan areas on the East Coast (Wilkerson, 2010). Since the beginning of the 20th century, during the Great Migration, thousands of Black/African American migrants from the South moved to inner cities in the North (Wilkerson, 2010). At the end of World War II, millions of GIs returned home and started a national baby boom, further increasing demand for habitable housing (Von Hoffman, 2003). Real estate developer Levitt & Sons noticed this rapid increase in demand, took advantage of the FHA Loan Guaranty and the VA Loan Guaranty programs, and successfully pioneered assembly line construction without union labor to build fully furnished, modestly priced housing in Levittown near Hempstead on Long Island (Jackson, 1985). This development strategy spread rapidly all over the U.S. (Jackson, 1985).

Many middle-income (typically non-Hispanic White) homebuyers took advantage of the policies and programs passed during the Great Depression and World War II and moved to the suburbs, while most low-income renters (typically of color), who were locked out of the same policies and programs, remained in inner cities (Von Hoffman, 2003). Some unscrupulous realtors furthered so-called *White Flight* by *blockbusting*, convincing non-Hispanic White homeowners to sell their homes due to fear of in-moving Blacks/African Americans, while also persuading Blacks/African Americans to move to the vacated homes (Austen, 2018). The so-called White Flight led to residential *racial and ethnic segregation*, causing inner cities to become disproportionately Black/African American and suburbs to remain disproportionately non-Hispanic White ("chocolate cities, vanilla suburbs") (Farley et al., 1978). The policies and programs passed during the Great Depression and World War II thus accelerated the abandonment and the economic decline of older industrial inner cities in future decades (Dreier et al., 2014).

While the overall nationwide shortage of habitable and affordable housing was partially alleviated through the construction boom in the suburbs, the increase in housing demand was larger than the increase in housing supply in the inner cities (Rothstein, 2017). Thus, in the late 1940s and mid-1950s, Congress passed the *Housing Acts of 1949 and 1954*, which authorized slum clearance and urban renewal that resulted in massive displacement, especially for people of color in inner cities, but implicitly facilitated homeownership, especially for non-Hispanic White people in the suburbs (Howard, 2013). The *Housing Act of 1949* declared the following national housing policy:

> The general welfare and security of the Nation and the health and living standards of its people require housing production and related community development sufficient to remedy the serious housing shortage, the elimination of sub-standard and other inadequate housing through the clearance of slums and blighted areas, and the realization as soon as feasible of the goal of a decent home and suitable living environment for every American family, thus contributing to the development and redevelopment of communities and to the advancement of the growth, wealth, and security of the Nation.
>
> (Housing Act of 1949 (Section 2 and Title V))

This Act was focused on residential development (Caves, 2012b). Among other aspects, *Title I* focused on inner cities and authorized the Slum Clearance and *Community Development* program, stipulating that public housing should be built in close proximity to razed developments, thus preventing it from being built in the suburbs and also mollifying the real estate industry (Bloom & Lasner, 2016; Caves, 2012a, 2012b; Plunz, 2016; Rohe, 2012). *Title II* focused on suburbs and extended and increased FHA insurance for homeowners, broadening homeownership to low-income, typically non-Hispanic White homebuyers, while also establishing FHA insurance for multifamily developments (Bloom & Lasner, 2016; Caves, 2012a, 2012b; Heathcott, 2015; Plunz, 2016; Rohe, 2012). *Title III* focused on inner cities and had the goal of constructing 810,000 low-rent public housing units within six years to replace the units torn down through urban renewal (Caves, 2012a; Heathcott, 2015).

The *Housing Act of 1954* changed the program title of the Slum Clearance and Urban Redevelopment program to the Slum Clearance and Urban Renewal program and provided two-thirds of the cost for approved neighborhood development projects, while cities paid the remaining third (Caves, 2012b). This Act was not only focused on residential but also on commercial and institutional development, redevelopment, and rehabilitation (Howard, 2013). Among other aspects, the Act authorized two mortgage insurance programs for homeowners. *Section 220* authorized FHA mortgage insurance for rehabilitating existing and constructing new buildings in urban renewal areas (Caves, 2012b). *Section 221(d)(2)* provided FHA mortgage insurance for low- and moderate-income households, typically non-Hispanic White, and in particular those displaced by urban renewal activities (Caves, 2012b).

Based on national security concerns, including the fear of a nuclear attack that would affect dense cities the most, Congress passed the *Federal-Aid Highway Act of 1956*, which authorized highway construction that not only connected metropolitan areas but also facilitated the commute from residential suburbs, facilitated by the gradual increase in car ownership, to employment centers in inner cities, which perpetuated the so-called White flight to the suburbs. Until the 1970s, most households of color remained in central cities, which experienced losses of jobs in manufacturing (Willse, 2015). Since the 1950s, many employers had followed the out-movers to the suburbs, increasing the attraction of homeownership for many (Kramer et al., 2008; Mendenhall, 2018, n.p.).

The *Housing and Urban Development Act of 1968* introduced the *Section 235 Homeownership Program*, which offered low down payment, low-interest mortgages to eligible homebuyers who had modest incomes and were unable to meet the FHA requirements in return for a monthly mortgage insurance premium (Rohe, 2012; Taylor, 2019). The subsidy covered the difference between the regular interest rate in the FHA mortgage insurance program and a reduced interest rate of as low as 1% (Federal Register, 2015). Proponents of Section 235 argued that this program stabilized neighborhoods, prevented urban uprisings, and promoted virtue (Anonymous, 1995). Opponents criticized Ginnie Mae for disbursing mortgage principal and interest payments directly to lenders and developers, some of which cut corners during construction, resulting in increased profit for them but high expenditures for major repairs for borrowers (Highsmith, 2015). Section 235 was terminated in 1988 (Federal Register, 2015).

8.3 HOUSING POLICY AND THE GREAT RECESSION

In the 1980s and 1990s, the lending industry advocated market deregulation (e.g., the elimination of state usury laws that had capped interest rates), mortgage product and technical innovation (e.g., subprime mortgages), and risk-based pricing (i.e., borrowers with a higher credit risk paying higher interest and fees in exchange for subprime mortgages) (Schwartz, 2021). Thus, Congress passed two Acts that regulated risk-based pricing: *The Depository Institutions Deregulation and Monetary Control Act*, passed in 1980, gave lenders the flexibility to set rates and fees for mortgages and the *Alternative Mortgage Transaction Parity Act*, passed in 1982, allowed lenders to create variable-rate mortgages and mortgages with balloon payments. These trends have become more common since the 1990s and have led to affordable but not necessarily sustainable homeownership for those who had been previously left out of homeownership, as witnessed during the Great Recession (Anacker & Crossney, 2013).

In 1990, Congress passed the *HOME Investment Partnerships Program*, enacting $1.35 billion in Fiscal Year (FY) 2021 (U.S. Department of Housing and Urban Development, n.d.b, 2023b). The goal of this program is to increase the supply of decent, safe, and affordable housing by acquiring, rehabilitating, and constructing housing and to assist low-income homebuyers who may have household incomes at or below 80% of the AMI (New York State, n.d.). Between 1992 and 2023, the HOME Program funded about 1.36 million housing units (National Council of State Housing Agencies, n.d.).

The *Federal Housing Enterprises Financial Safety and Soundness Act of 1992*, amended by the *Housing and Economic Recovery Act of 2008*, specifies affordable single-family housing goals for Fannie Mae and Freddie Mac (Federal Housing Finance Agency, n.d.b). The three single-family home *purchase* housing goals are based on the percentage of the total number of home purchase mortgages that Fannie Mae and Freddie Mac each purchase every year. They fall into three categories: (1) low-income households with an income of less than 80% of the AMI; (2) very low-income households with an income of less than 50% of the AMI; and (3) households in low-income areas ("Duty to Serve") (Federal Housing Finance Agency, n.d.b). The single-purchase *refinance* housing goal is based on the percentage of the total number of refinance mortgages that Fannie Mae and Freddie Mac each refinance every year for households with an income of less than 80% of the AMI (Federal Housing Finance Agency, n.d.b). The Federal Housing Finance Agency sets the annual benchmark for each category before the calendar year starts and then compares and contrasts that benchmark with the actual market and the performance of Fannie Mae and Freddie Mac after the year is over.

For example, the established benchmark for the low-income borrower home purchase proportion was 24% in 2021, while the actual market was 26.7%, Fannie Mae's performance was 28.7% (i.e., surpassing the benchmark), and Freddie Mac's performance was 27.4% (i.e., also surpassing the benchmark) (Federal Housing Finance Agency, n.d.c). The benchmark set for the very low-income borrower home purchase proportion was 6%, while the actual market was 6.8%, Fannie Mae's performance was 7.4%, but Freddie Mac's performance was only 6.3% (Federal Housing Finance Agency, n.d.c). Next, the established benchmark for the low-income home purchase proportion was 14%, the actual market was 19.1%, Fannie Mae's performance was 20.3%, but Freddie Mac's performance was only 18.0% (Federal Housing Finance Agency, n.d.c). Lastly, the benchmark set for the low-income borrower refinance share was 21%, the actual market was 26.1%, Fannie Mae's performance was 26.2%, and Freddie Mac's performance was 24.8% (i.e., the latter did not meet the benchmark) (Federal Housing Finance Agency, n.d.c).

During the Great Recession, many borrowers and lenders disproportionately utilized these policies and programs to weather the national foreclosure crisis that resulted in about 2.8 million foreclosure filings; the house price crisis in which house prices declined about 33% from the peak in 2006 to the trough in 2012; the underwater crisis that left more than 30% of home mortgages with a higher debt than the market value; the financial and banking crises that resulted in 489 failed banks from 2008 to 2013; the economic crisis that technically lasted 18 months and had a cumulative GDP loss of 4.1%; and the unemployment crisis, in which the unemployment rate peaked at 10% in October 2009 (Anonymous, 2010a, 2010b; Attom Data Solutions, 2019; Boushey et al., 2019; Goodman et al., 2017; National Bureau of Economic Research, n.d.; National Commission on the Causes of the Financial and Economic Crisis in the United States, 2011; Zillow, 2012).

During the Great Recession, the FHLB system, which consists of highly leveraged financial institutions with relatively small capital buffers, stabilized the financial system as the "lender of next-to-last resort" (Gissler & Narajabad, 2017a, n.p.). For example, between 2007 and the fall of 2008, FHLB's wholesale funding to member banks increased by 50% while interest income decreased significantly, illustrating both members' challenges in accessing other sources of funding and a severe funding crunch (Gissler & Narajabad, 2017b, 2017c). As part of the *Housing and Economic Recovery Act (HERA)* of 2008, Congress changed the overseer of the FHLB system from the Federal Housing Finance Board (FHFB) to the FHFA (Federal Housing Finance Agency, n.d.a).

The HOLC was dissolved in 1954, and a successor to take on mortgage modifications of distressed borrowers could have been a newly established unit under the Consumer Financial Protection Bureau (CFPB). In 2007, at the beginning of the national foreclosure crisis, Warren (2007, n.p.) argued that:

> [i]t is impossible to buy a toaster that has a one-in-five chance of bursting into flames and burning down your house. But it is possible to refinance an existing home with a mortgage that has the same one-in-five chance of putting the family out on the street.

Thus, she advocated for a Financial Product Safety Commission, modeled after the U.S. Consumer Product Safety Commission, an independent agency of the U.S. government (Kirsch & Squires, 2017). Indeed, the Dodd-Frank Wall Street Reform and Consumer Protection Act (Dodd-Frank Act) established the CFPB in 2010, and it formally began operations in July 2011, well after the peak of the 2010 national foreclosure crisis (Anonymous, 2010a, 2010b; Federal Register, 2019; RealtyTrac, 2013). Since then, the CFPB has intensified its focus on consumer protections, trying to find the right balance between educating consumers and limiting their choices and reinventing bank regulations (Mogilnicki & Malpass, 2013; Skeel, 2011).

In the meantime, Congress created several programs in the late 2000s that fall into two categories: (1) programs that prevented or reduced foreclosures, and (2) programs that mitigated the impacts of foreclosures on neighborhoods (Immergluck, 2013). Congress could have done so, but chose not to relaunch HOLC (Glantz, 2019). Immergluck (2013), among many others, argued that the federal response to the foreclosure crisis had been "too little, too late, and too timid." Examples of programs that fall into the first category are the *FHA Secure* program, the *National Foreclosure Mitigation Counseling (NFMC)* program, the *Hope for Homeowners (H4H)* program, and the *Making Home Affordable (MHA)* program, along with its many ancillary programs. An example of a program that falls into the second category is the *Neighborhood Stabilization Programs (NSPs)*. In addition to these public programs, there was also the *Hope Now Alliance*, which included banks, lenders, and nonprofit organizations that offered free foreclosure prevention counseling via a 1–800 number, and the *American Securitization Forum*, a trade group consisting of structured finance investors who worked on streamlining voluntary modifications of subprime mortgages (Immergluck, 2013).

One of the programs that prevented or reduced foreclosures was the *FHA Secure* program, which was launched in August 2007 to allow any borrower to refinance their mortgage but was terminated in December 2008 to prevent a negative impact on the FHA's Mutual Mortgage Insurance (MMI) Fund (U.S. Department of Housing and Urban Development, 2008). By the end of March 2008, only 1,729 delinquent mortgages had been refinanced (Swarns, 2008).

A second program, the *National Foreclosure Mitigation Counseling (NFMC)* program, was launched in January 2008 to fund housing counseling organizations to advise borrowers at risk of foreclosure until it ended in December 2018 (Scally, Gold, & DuBois, 2018). The NFMC program funded counseling to about 2.14 million borrowers for $853.1 million appropriated by Congress (Scally, Gold, & DuBois, 2018).

A third program, the *Hope for Homeowners (H4H)* program, based on the *Emergency Economic Stabilization Act (EESA)* of 2008 and backed by the FHA, allowed eligible distressed borrowers to refinance their FHA-insured mortgages in return for lowered principal amounts and the elimination of junior (i.e., subordinate) liens (Engel & McCoy, 2011). It operated from October 1, 2008 to September 30, 2011 (U.S. Department of Housing and Urban Development, 2010). However, only 340 loans were refinanced in Fiscal Year (FY) 2010 (Immergluck, 2013). Engel and McCoy (2011) explained that H4H failed because lenders were unwilling to reduce principal amounts and investors and servicers were unwilling to eliminate any junior liens on properties.

A fourth program that prevented or reduced foreclosures was the *Making Home Affordable (MHA)* program, consisting of several programs, which was established by the U.S. Department of the Treasury in February 2009 and ended in December 2016. One of the programs was the *Home Affordable Mortgage Program (HAMP)*, which incentivized servicers to modify mortgages of eligible borrowers who were at least 60 days delinquent or at risk of default, achieving a monthly mortgage payment of less than 31% of their gross monthly income (Engel & McCoy, 2011). Eligible borrowers needed to be owner-occupiers, have a debt-to-income ratio of over 31%, and have a mortgage with a first lien and a total mortgage amount of less than $729,750 (Engel & McCoy, 2011). Servicers that had received more than two rounds of Troubled Asset Relief Program (TARP) funds and serviced loans guaranteed by Fannie Mae or Freddie Mac were required to participate in HAMP (Engel & McCoy, 2011). Other servicers were encouraged to participate, and the participation rate was about 85% (Engel & McCoy, 2011). Participating servicers received $1,000 for each mortgage modification and an additional $1,000 per year if the borrower did not default for up to three years (Engel & McCoy, 2011). Participating borrowers received $1,000 per year if they did not redefault for up to five years (Engel & McCoy, 2011). Initially, the U.S. Department of the Treasury had the goal to modify 3 to 4 million mortgages by the original deadline of December 31, 2012, extended to December 31, 2016 (Whelan, 2018). However, only 1.7 million mortgages were modified, and there were still about 645,000 participating borrowers in the program as of June 2021 (Special Inspector General for the Troubled Asset Relief Program, 2021). There are several reasons for the somewhat low number of borrowers served. Treasury issued guidelines and distributed monies to mortgage servicers, which were tasked with deciding on mortgage modifications (Whelan, 2018). For example, JPMorgan Chase Bank, Citibank, and Bank of America had rejected at least 80% of HAMP applications by April 2015 (Whelan, 2018). Thus, many of these borrowers were forced to foreclose.

Another MHA program was the *Home Affordable Refinance Program (HARP)*, in which borrowers with mortgages guaranteed or owned by Fannie Mae or Freddie Mac before June 1, 2009, strong payment histories, and loan-to-value (LTV) ratios above 80% were eligible to refinance them into low-interest, fixed-rate mortgages (Engel & McCoy, 2011). HARP ran from April 1, 2009 to December 31, 2018 (Abel & Fuster, 2021). In mid-2012, the Treasury reformed HARP, eliminating the LTV ratio cap, leading to a wave of further modifications in 2012 and 2013 (Abel & Fuster, 2021). By the end of the program, the Treasury had made about 3.5 million mortgage modifications under the MHA program, resulting in an average reduced monthly payment of about $175 (or 11%) and a 40% lower likelihood of default (Abel & Fuster, 2021).

The three *Neighborhood Stabilization Programs (NSPs)* also mitigated the impacts of foreclosures on neighborhoods, providing emergency assistance to state and local governments, nonprofit organizations, and consortia of nonprofit entities to stabilize eligible communities that had high rates of abandoned and foreclosed homes (U.S. Department of Housing and Urban Development, n.d.i). These programs were administered in three rounds. *NSP 1* awarded $3.92 billion to 307 and *NSP 3* awarded $1 billion to 270 state and local governments, respectively, based on award formula bases (U.S. Department of Housing and Urban Development, n.d.i). *NSP 2* provided $2.0 billion to 56 states, local governments, nonprofit organizations, and consortia of nonprofit entities, based on a competitive basis (U.S. Department of Housing and Urban Development, n.d.i). The funding for NSP 1, based on HERA of 2008, started in March 2009 and ended in March 2013 (NSP Questions @ HUD.gov, email correspondence, November 26, 2019). The funding for NSP 2, authorized by the *American Recovery and Reinvestment Act (ARRA)* of 2009, began in February 2010 and ended in February

2013 (NSP Questions @ HUD.gov, email correspondence, November 26, 2019). Finally, the funding for NSP 3, based on the Dodd-Frank Wall Street Reform and Consumer Protection Act of 2010, began in March 2011 and ended in April 2014 (Dodd-Frank Act) (Anonymous, 2010a, 2010b; Federal Register, 2019; NSP Questions @ HUD.gov, email correspondence, November 26, 2019). Immergluck (2013) argued that the relatively narrow NSP 1 legislation hindered an effective and opportunistic response by grantees, although NSPs 2 and 3 were somewhat more flexible. He concluded that the federal government's response to the foreclosure crisis included programs that were tentative, incremental, marginal, clumsy, and difficult to implement at scale (Immergluck, 2013).

In addition to the many programs established by several Acts in the late 2000s, the *2010 Dodd-Frank Act* also expanded the FDIC's powers and responsibilities, including by increasing the deposit guarantee from $100,000 to $250,000 and continuing and expanding its supervision of banks, the management of the Deposit Insurance Fund, and the resolution of large banks that had failed, including IndyMac, Washington Mutual, and many small community banks (Carns, 2017; Clements, 2023; Hashimzade et al., 2017).

The FDIC implemented its deposit guarantee, supervision of banks, and resolution of failed banks during four of the largest bank failures in U.S. history that occurred in March and May of 2023, possibly indicating a contagion effect that was facilitated by social media and the 24/7 news cycle (Clements, 2023; Gruenberg, 2023). The failures revealed traditional banking challenges, such as a lack of portfolio diversification, maturity mismatches (i.e., borrowing short and lending long), inflation, an increase in interest rates, and geopolitical uncertainties (Blinder, 2014; Geithner, 2014; Gruenberg, 2023; Reinhart & Rogoff, 2009). These failures also showed current challenges, such as inflation, rapid portfolio growth, and investments in digital assets (Bernanke et al., 2020; Gruenberg, 2023). The recent failures may have impacted the stability of the financial market, including the stability of the housing finance market, as lenders may have decreased their risk tolerance, either by reducing their lending activities or by increasing their interest rates or collateral requirements, among other strategies, resulting in a negatively impacted economy (Gruenberg, 2023; Santarelli, 2023).

The first bank to fail, *Silvergate Bank* in La Jolla, California, announced on March 8, 2023 that it would wind down operations and voluntarily liquidate, supervised by the California Department of Financial Protection and Innovation (Berry, 2023; Gruenberg, 2023). It had about $11.3 billion in assets as of late 2022 and primarily serviced digital asset companies (Gruenberg, 2023). In November 2022, digital asset exchange FTX collapsed and Silvergate Bank subsequently explained that less than 10% of its deposits were housed at FTX (Gruenberg, 2023). Nevertheless, a bank run occurred shortly thereafter, resulting in an earnings loss of $1 billion and a severe decline of its stock price (Gruenberg, 2023). As of this writing, Silvergate Bank announced that it intended to fully repay deposits on March 8, 2023 (Lang & Chakroborti, 2023).

Second, the *Silicon Valley Bank (SVB)* in Santa Clara, California, then the 16th largest bank by asset value, with about $209 billion in assets and about $175 billion in deposits as of late 2022, failed on March 10, 2023 (Clements, 2023; Gruenberg, 2023). SVB's customers had primarily been technology, health care, and private equity entrepreneurs, many of them small- and medium-sized businesses (Clements, 2023; Gruenberg, 2023). About 15% of SVB's loan portfolio consisted of residential and commercial mortgages (Tracey, 2023). Risky business activities, ineffective risk management, and the relatively fast end of the very long period of very low interest rates contributed to SVB's failure. In terms of business activities, SVB's assets had increased from $56 billion to $209 billion (198%) from December 2018 to December 2022, compared with 33% for the median total assets of peer banks (Clements, 2023; Gruenberg, 2023). This growth in assets primarily occurred through uninsured deposits (i.e., deposits higher than the $250,000 FDIC insurance limit), which constituted 70–80% of the bank's total assets, compared with 31–41% for banks of similar size between 2018 to 2022 (Clements, 2023). In terms of risk management, SVB's past lower-yielding securities lost value when interest rates increased nationwide in 2022 and 2023 (Clements, 2023). Thus, the Federal Reserve Bank of San Francisco downgraded SVB's rating in June 2022 and announced (but did not finalize) intervention in August 2022 (Clements, 2023). On March 8, 2023, when Silvergate Bank announced its voluntary liquidation, it stated that it had just sold $1.8 billion of its securities portfolio while trying to raise $2.25 billion in capital (Gruenberg, 2023). Thus, depositors became concerned about the security of their funds and withdrew them in a bank run on March 9, 2023 (Gruenberg, 2023). SVB tried to cover the remaining deposits, selling the lower-yielding securities at huge losses before eventually failing. The California Department of Financial Protection and Innovation closed SVB on March 10, 2023, stating insufficient liquidity and solvency, and simultaneously appointed the FDIC as the receiver of the bank (Clements, 2023; Gruenberg, 2023). The FDIC subsequently transferred the Bank's deposits to a bridge bank it had established a few days later and then signed a purchase agreement for all deposits and loans with First-Citizens Bank & Trust Company in Raleigh, North Carolina, on March 26, 2023 (Federal Deposit Insurance Corporation, n.d.c; Gruenberg, 2023).

Third, *Signature Bank* in New York City, then the 29th largest bank by asset value, with about $110 billion in assets and almost $89 billion in deposits as of late 2022, failed on March 12, 2023 (Clements, 2023; Gruenberg, 2023). Signature Bank's customers had primarily been in commercial real estate and multifamily housing, many of them small- and medium-sized businesses (Clements, 2023; Gruenberg, 2023). Similar to SVB, Signature Bank faced challenges in business activities and risk management. In terms of business activities, Signature Bank's assets had increased from $47 to $110 billion (134%) from December 2018 to December 2022, constituting 63–82% of its total assets between 2018 and 2022 (Clements, 2023). In terms of risk management, Signature Bank had relied on uninsured deposits, but also expanded its activities in the digital asset industry (e.g., cryptocurrency), which became increasingly volatile in 2022 (Clements, 2023). That year, the FDIC considered increasing supervisory actions and eventually downgraded the bank's rating on March 11, 2023 (Clements, 2023). When Signature Bank customers with large deposits learned about SVB's failure, they became concerned about the security of their deposits and withdrew them in a bank run (Clements, 2023). The New York State Department of Financial Services closed Signature Bank, stating low liquidity and management challenges, and simultaneously appointed the FDIC as the receiver on March 12, 2023 (Clements, 2023; Gruenberg, 2023). The FDIC subsequently signed a purchase agreement for almost all deposits and select loans with Flagstar Bank, NA, in Hicksville, New York, on March 19, 2023 (Clements, 2023; Gruenberg, 2023).

Fourth, FDIC closed *First Republic Bank* in San Francisco, which had about $229 billion in assets and almost $104 billion in deposits, on May 1, 2023 (Federal Deposit Insurance Corporation, n.d.c). In late 2022, almost 68% of its deposits were uninsured and its loan-to-deposit ratio was 111% (i.e., there were more loans than deposits; Gura, 2023). In mid-March 2023, 11 financial institutions deposited $30 billion in First Republic Bank to shore up declining confidence after its credit rating was downgraded and when its share values were volatile during bank runs, discussed above (Egan et al., 2023; Gura, 2023). On May 1, 2023, JP Morgan Chase Bank, NA assumed all deposits and almost all assets of this bank (Federal Deposit Insurance Corporation, n.d.c).

In an unusual step, U.S. Treasury allowed the FDIC to utilize its emergency systematic risk authorities under the Federal Deposit Insurance Act in March 2023, protecting *all depositors* of the SVB and Signature Bank, regardless of whether they were insured (i.e., had deposits below $250,000) or uninsured (i.e., had deposits above $250,000; Gruenberg, 2023). By contrast, shareholders and unsecured *creditors* lost their investments (Gruenberg, 2023).

URBAN HOUSING POLICY AND OWNER-OCCUPIED HOUSING

9.1 MORTGAGE INTEREST DEDUCTION (MID)

Homeownership has been supported by *tax policy through deductions, exemptions, and tax credits* for more than a century in the U.S. (Schwartz, 2021). From 1913 until 1986, 26 U.S.C. § 163(h) of the Internal Revenue Code allowed deduction of property taxes, as well as interest on mortgages, personal loans, and credit card debt (Geisst, 2017). In the first half of the 20th century, the U.S. home-ownership rate was less than 50%, so only a very small proportion of borrowers deducted property taxes and mortgage interest (Bourassa & Grigsby, 2000). During World War II, property tax rates skyrocketed, increasing the proportion of borrowers who deducted their property taxes and mortgage interest payments (Bourassa & Grigsby, 2000). The *Tax Reform Act of 1986* limited these deductions, allowing only property taxes and interest on mortgages for the first $1 million of primary or secondary residences for joint filers to be deducted (Bourassa & Grigsby, 2000; Keightley, 2020). In sum, the mortgage interest deduction facilitated home-ownership from the second half of the 20th century until 2017, and to a lesser degree after December 2017, when the *Tax Cut and Jobs Act (TCJA)* was passed (Keightley, 2020). However, the TCJA will expire after 2025 (Keightley, 2020).

The *reformed MID* allows those with a primary residence or a second home who have a mortgage debt of less than $750,000 for joint filers (or $375,000 for single or separate filers) to itemize qualified

DOI: 10.1201/9781032657646-12

expenses, including their property taxes and mortgage interest payments (Internal Revenue Service, n.d.). These qualified expenses need to be higher than the standard deduction amount for joint ($25,900 in 2022) and single filers ($12,950 in 2022) under the age of 65 (Internal Revenue Service, n.d.). In Fiscal Year (FY) 2018, the MID was the largest source of support ($85.8 billion total, or about 85%) of all tax expenditures for housing (about $101.1 billion total) (Schwartz, 2021).

Interestingly, the MID has disproportionately benefited higher-income instead of lower-income borrowers for three reasons (Keightley, 2020). First, higher-income borrowers tend to itemize their eligible expenditures, unlike lower-income borrowers (Keightley, 2020). For example, 37.3% of households with an annual household income above $200,000 itemized expenditures in 2018, compared to 3.0% of households with an income of less than $50,000 (Tax Policy Center, 2018; the most recent information as of this writing). Second, higher-income households have higher marginal tax rates and thus higher eligible expenditures (Keightley, 2020). Third, higher-income households tend to purchase homes with higher property values and may take out mortgages with higher amounts compared to lower-income households (Keightley, 2020). In sum, the MID has only had a modest impact on the home purchase decision of whether to own or rent and a small impact on the size of the home (Keightley, 2020). Indeed, some argue that the MID has contributed to economic, racial, and ethnic inequality. Non-Hispanic White households (constituting 66.1% of the entire population) received 70.9% of MID's benefits in 2018, while Black/African American households (12.5% of the population) received 7.7%, Hispanic/Latino households (13.9% of the population) received 10.3%, and Asian households (4.9% of the population) received 8.8% (Meschede et al., 2021). The larger proportion of non-Hispanic White and Asian households who take advantage of the MID may be attributed to larger household incomes and thus higher marginal tax rates, higher homeownership rates, and higher property values (Meschede et al., 2021).

9.2 FEDERAL HOUSING ADMINISTRATION (FHA)

During the Great Recession, the FHA's cross-subsidization principle, which has provided countercyclical and regional stabilization since its beginning, proved useful (Galante, 2013a, 2017). In *cross-subsidization*, the FHA's mortgage insurance premium (MIP) is based on the insurance pool, with the borrower paying a MIP to FHA's MMI Fund, the revenues of which are utilized to insure FHA mortgages that are in turn backed by the full faith and credit of the U.S. government (U.S. Department of Housing and Urban Development, n.d.g). The MIP is determined by the base loan amount (over/under $625,000), the term (less/more than 15 years), and the LTV ratio (i.e., the proportion of the loan of the base loan amount, including less than 90%, between 90% and less than 95%, and over 95%) (U.S. Department of Housing and Urban Development, 2017b). In other words, the MIP is not determined by credit risk (Bhutta & Ringo, 2016).

The MIP consists of a one-time, upfront premium (currently 1.75% of the base loan amount, although the premium can be rolled into the mortgage), as well as an annual premium over the life of the loan that ranges from 0.80% of the base loan amount (e.g., for a mortgage with a base loan amount of less than $625,500, a term of more than 15 years, and an LTV ratio of less than 95%) to 1.05% of the base loan amount (e.g., for a mortgage with a base loan amount of more than $625,000, a term of more than 15 years, and an LTV ratio of more than 95%) (U.S. Department of Housing and Urban Development, 2017b). The MIP may be lower or higher than private mortgage insurance (PMI) on conventional mortgages that have a loan-to-value ratio of more than 80%, depending on the risk profile of the borrower (Bhutta & Ringo, 2016). A typical first-year payment may be $1,890 for a $200,000 FHA-insured mortgage, with a 4% interest rate, a one-time upfront premium of 1.75%, and an annual premium of.85% of the base loan amount (Bhutta & Ringo, 2016).

The FHA has provided *countercyclical stabilization* during major recessions, including the Great Recession. For example, FHA's market share was 1.90% in 2005. It increased to 16.10% in 2008 and 17.90% in 2009; gradually declined to 14.90% in 2010, 13.09% in 2011, 11.38% in 2012, 11.07% in 2013, and 10.56% in 2014; increased to 13.90% in 2015, 12.36% in 2016, 13.08% in 2017, and then decreased thereafter, as shown in Figure 9.1 (U.S. Department of Housing and Urban Development, 2023c). The increase in FHA's market share from 2007 to 2011 can be attributed to conventional lenders retrenching from the mortgage market during and after the

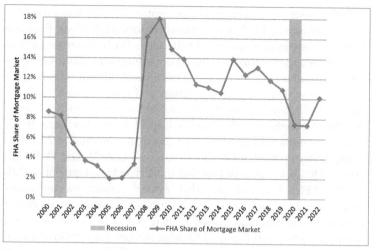

Figure 9.1 Market share of Federal Housing Administration (FHA), 2000–2022
Source: author, based on U.S. Department of Housing and Urban Development (2023c).

Great Recession (Galante, 2013b; Goodman et al., 2019a, 2019b; Griffith, 2012). The decrease in FHA's market share after 2019 can be attributed to borrowers flocking to conventional lenders after the Great Recession, once they welcomed business again. In addition to providing countercyclical stabilization, Moody's calculated that if FHA had not conducted any activities from October 2010 until December 2011, home prices would have decreased by an additional 25%, home sales would have declined by a further 40%, and new home construction would have decreased by an additional 60% (Galante, 2017). FHA activities prevented the unemployment rate from soaring to almost 12% and saved 3 million jobs and half a trillion dollars in economic output (Griffith, 2012).

In theory, the MMI Fund is funded by self-generated income and does not depend on taxpayers' money (U.S. Department of Housing and Urban Development, n.d.g). However, the MMI's Economic Net Worth Capital Ratio was below its statutorily mandated 2.0% minimum from 2009 to 2014 (U.S. Department of Housing and Urban Development, 2012, 2016). Based on the Federal Credit Reform Act of 1990 (FCRA), which requires that there must be sufficient reserves to cover 100% of estimated future losses over the next 30 years, the FHA was required to draw $1.7 billion from the U.S. Treasury in September 2013 (Riquier, 2017). Interestingly, this mandatory appropriation was based on assumptions about loan performance and recoveries made in December 2012, not reflecting the much better then-current and future performance, cash position, and the fiscal health of the MMI Fund in September 2013 (Galante, 2013b). Nevertheless, the MMI's Capital Ratio has been (well) above the minimum over the past few years, holding at 2.76% in 2018, 4.84% in 2019, 6.10% in 2020, 8.03% in 2021, and 11.11% in 2022 (U.S. Department of Housing and Urban Development, 2022).

The FHA has also provided *regional stabilization* by cross-subsidizing local housing markets through its uniform mortgage insurance premium rates, which are determined by outstanding loan amounts. Whereas some local housing markets have relatively high house prices and mortgage amounts and will thus command high FHA mortgage premia, others have relatively low house prices and mortgage amounts and will have low FHA mortgage premia. However, the risk is nevertheless borrower-dependent.

The FHA has also played a significant role in *relief and recovery efforts in Presidentially Declared Major Disaster Areas (PDMDAs)* in the U.S., including Puerto Rico (U.S. Department of Housing and Urban Development, 2021). As the number of hurricanes, wildfires, floods, and other natural disasters will increase in the future, FHA's role will also increase (U.S. Department of Housing and Urban Development, 2021).

Since the beginning of the Great Recession, the FHA has increasingly insured conventional mortgages disproportionately held by Black/African American and Hispanic/Latino borrowers (U.S. Department of Housing and Urban Development, 2022). For example, in Fiscal Year (FY) 2018, 12.63%, 18.18%, and 2.60% (33.41% in total) of borrowers of FHA-insured mortgages for purchase were Black/African American, Hispanic/Latino, and Asian, respectively, compared to 55.53% of non-Hispanic White borrowers (U.S. Department of Housing and Urban Development, 2022). Indeed, in calendar year 2018, 6.7%, 8.9%, and 5.9% (21.5% in total) of borrowers of mortgages for purchase recorded by the FFIEC were Black/African American, Hispanic/Latino, and Asian, respectively, compared to 62% of non-Hispanic White borrowers (Dietrich et al.,

2019). In sum, the FHA has served a relatively high proportion of Black/African American and Hispanic/Latino borrowers since the mid-2010s, which is a huge change from the 1960s.

9.3 FANNIE MAE AND FREDDIE MAC

During the subprime, foreclosure, and economic crises, Fannie Mae and Freddie Mac faced enormous pressures (Howard, 2014). Although these two government-sponsored enterprises (GSEs) had largely remained on the sidelines with respect to the purchase and securitization of subprime loans, they did purchase bonds backed by poorly underwritten subprime loans and later securitized high-risk Alt-A prime mortgages of borrowers who did not provide full documentation (Howard, 2014). These bonds eventually defaulted and contributed to huge losses for both GSEs (Scharfstein & Sunderam, 2011). Thus, the U.S. Department of the Treasury established the Federal Housing Finance Agency (FHFA) in July 2008 to place Fannie Mae and Freddie Mac into conservatorship in September 2008 in order to enact "a process in which the government holds a failed financial institution with the purpose of restoring the firm to solvency" (Stanton, 2012, p. 245).

In other words, the *implicit federal guarantee* now became *explicit*, as the federal government guaranteed principal and interest payments on mortgage-backed securities (MBSs) held by Fannie Mae and Freddie Mac and bailed out the two GSEs (Bernanke, 2022). During the financial crisis, Fannie Mae and Freddie Mac drew $119.8 billion and $48.1 billion, respectively (Ramirez, 2019a, 2019b). In return, the federal government mandated that the two GSEs first send 10% of their profits (in 2009, called "profit sweep") and then their entire profits (after 2012, called "net worth sweep") to the Treasury, ensuring that there was sufficient capital to bail them out again in case of another future housing crisis (Lane, 2019). After a few years, Fannie Mae and Freddie Mac became profitable, eventually repaying a total of $181.4 billion and $119.7 billion to the Treasury, respectively (Ramirez, 2019b). Thus, the two GSEs paid $133.2 billion in total *beyond the bailout* they had received during the Great Recession. Recently, shareholders of Fannie Mae and Freddie Mac sued the Secretary of the U.S. Department of Treasury, as they disagreed with the "net worth sweep" that denied them dividends (Weinstein,

2019). In September 2019, shareholders won the case, which ruled that the "net worth sweep" was illegal (*Collins v. Mnuchin, 2019*). As of this writing, the question of what remedy the shareholders of Fannie Mae and Freddie Mac are entitled to remains open.

In September 2019, the federal government allowed Fannie Mac and Freddie Mac to prepare for an exit from conservatorship by rebuilding a portion of their capital reserves to a combined total of $45 billion (Ramirez, 2019b). The FHFA's next step is to reform housing finance by privatizing the two GSEs, limiting the role of the government in housing finance while increasing marketplace competition (Ramirez, 2019a, 2019b). However, it remains to be seen whether Fannie Mae and Freddie Mac will support affordable housing and sustainable homeownership and whether the housing finance market will provide options to address a potential recession.

In sum, many borrowers have gained access to affordable and sustainable homeownership over the past eight decades through the following public and semipublic institutions, policies, and programs:

- the Federal Home Loan Bank (FHLB) system;
- the Home Owners' Loan Corporation (HOLC);
- the Federal Deposit Insurance Corporation (FDIC);
- the FHA;
- Fannie Mae;
- the VA Loan Guaranty;
- the Housing Acts of 1949 and 1954;
- Executive Order #11063;
- the Fair Housing Act of 1968 and 1988;
- the Housing and Urban Development Act of 1968;
- the Equal Credit Opportunity Act (ECOA) of 1974;
- the Home Mortgage Disclosure Act (HMDA) of 1975;
- the Community Reinvestment Act (CRA) of 1977;
- the HOME Investment Partnerships Program; and
- the Federal Housing Enterprises Financial Safety and Soundness Act of 1992.

Currently, more than 75% of borrowers have financed their mortgages through Fannie Mae, Freddie Mac, the FHA, or the VA (Rothstein, 2023). Many borrowers have also gained access to sustainable homeownership through private institutions, such as lenders, credit bureaus and their credit scoring systems, the Federal Reserve System, and Wall Street, all discussed above.

All of these institutions, policies, and programs have led to a *national* homeownership rate that increased from 45.6% in 1920 to 66.6% in 2020. However, compared to select countries that are part of the Organisation for Economic Co-operation and Development (OECD), the United States' homeownership rate ranks in the lower middle. For example, Spain (78.2%), the Czech Republic (78.0%), Slovenia (76.2%), Italy (72.9%), Finland (72.7%), Mexico (71.7%), Sweden (70.6%), Ireland (70.0%), and Canada (67.0%) all had higher homeownership rates in 2015, whereas the United Kingdom (63.5%), Denmark (62.7%), Germany (51.9%), and Switzerland (51.3%) had lower homeownership rates (Goodman & Mayer, 2018). These differences may be attributed to economic, legal, institutional, or cultural differences, including the long-term reluctance of many U.S. municipalities to open neighborhoods zoned for single-family homes to more housing types, including duplexes, triplexes, or Accessory Dwelling Units (ADUs) (Anacker & Niedt, 2023; Bull & Gross, 2023; Whittemore & Curran-Groome, 2022).

Also, structural and individual factors have caused large discrepancies in the homeownership rate among racial and ethnic groups in the U.S. (U.S. Bureau of the Census, n.d.c). For example, non-Hispanic Whites had a homeownership rate of 74.4%, Blacks/African Americans had a homeownership rate of 45.9%, and Hispanics/Latinos had a homeownership rate of 48.6% in 2022 (U.S. Bureau of the Census, 2023). Given the increase in racial and ethnic diversity in the future, as discussed above, some policymakers, scholars, and professionals have presented many suggestions on how to close these lingering discrepancies (Graves et al., 2020).

10

URBAN HOUSING POLICY AND RENTER-OCCUPIED HOUSING

In addition to the many policies and programs that benefited home-owners, borrowers, and housing providers, the U.S. Congress has passed several policies and programs benefiting both low- and moderate-income renters and developers and providers of rental housing.

Policies and programs that benefit low- and moderate-income renters may be differentiated between *place-based programs* and *people-based programs*. Place-based programs include those administered by the U.S. Department of Housing and Urban Development (HUD) or the Federal Housing Administration (FHA):

*   HUD's public housing program since 1937;
*   HUD's Homeownership Opportunities for People Everywhere (HOPE VI) program from 1993 to 2010 in connection with public housing transformation;
*   HUD's Choice Neighborhoods program since 2010;
*   HUD's Rental Assistance Demonstration (RAD) program since 2013 (Weicher, 2012);
*   the FHA's Section 221(d)(3) Below Market Interest Rate (BMIR) program from 1961 to 1968;
*   the FHA's Section 236 program from 1968 to 1974;
*   HUD's CDBG program since 1974;
*   HUD's Section 8 New Construction and Substantial Rehabilitation (NC/SR) program from 1974 to 1983; and
*   the Internal Revenue Service's LIHTC program since 1986 (Stout et al., 2019).

DOI: 10.1201/9781032657646-13

People-based programs include HUD's Section 8 Voucher/Housing Choice Voucher (HCV) programs since 1974 (Stout et al., 2019).

10.1 PLACE-BASED PROGRAMS

Several Acts have authorized the public housing program, the first major federal housing program geared toward providing decent, affordable housing to low-income households: the *U.S. Housing Act of 1937*, the *Housing Act of 1949*, the *Housing Act of 1954*, and the *Housing and Urban Development Act of 1968* (Austen, 2018). The *U.S. Housing Act of 1937* (Section 9), also called the Wagner-Steagall Act, authorized the public housing program, which was the first major federal housing program geared toward very low-income households (Bratt, 2012). The Act had the goals of stimulating the economy, lowering the unemployment rate, and addressing decades-old housing challenges, including unsafe and unsanitary existing dwellings and the shortage of decent, safe, and affordable dwellings, all through housing construction (Austen, 2018). The Housing Act of 1937 limited the price per square foot for the building and the land that local public housing authorities (PHAs) were allowed to pay (Vale, 2000). Nevertheless, many considered the first public housing developments to be superior because the units had heat, electricity, and hot and cold running water; attractive amenities, such as refrigerators; and spacious, clean, and nicely landscaped sites (Freeman, 2019). Also, the Act only funded capital costs, or the principal on interest on bonds issued by the PHAs, which operate, maintain, and manage the units based on rental revenues (Austen, 2018). However, shortly after the public housing program started, the U.S. entered World War II (Austen, 2018). Thus, construction materials and activities were diverted to build homes for workers in war-related industries (Peterson, 2013).

While the *Housing Act of 1949* focused on residential development, the *Housing Act of 1954* also focused on commercial and institutional development. Due to the change in focus, and as Congress typically funded fewer units than authorized, the goal of constructing 810,000 units was delayed until 1968 (Caves, 2012a, 2012b). The *Housing and Urban Development Act of 1968* established a national goal of constructing or rehabilitating 26 million housing units through public and private sector production until 1978, with six of the 26 million reserved for low- and moderate-income families (Caves, 2012c). However, this goal was not met because of community resistance to public housing in the late 1960s and President Richard Nixon's moratorium in 1973 (McGhee, 2018).

Several national, state, and local private special interest associations in the construction and real estate sectors opposed the Acts, arguing that public housing should not compete against market-rate housing (Bratt, 2012). Thus, most public housing projects were built in low-income neighborhoods, often on sites that had previously been torn down in connection with urban renewal in the 1940s, 1950s, and 1960s and contributing to residential racial and ethnic segregation that has continued to persist, as evidenced in the Gautreaux case when Black/African American public housing tenants, led by Dorothy Gautreaux, sued the Chicago Housing Authority (CHA) and thus HUD in 1976, alleging that CHA had deliberately sited public housing in Chicago, avoiding potential resident backlash in non-Hispanic White neighborhoods (Vale, 2000).

In the past, most albeit not all public housing units were subject to severe cost constraints, resulting in a drab and monotonous appearance, challenged design aspects (e.g., broad "sidewalk in the sky" galleries that faced increasing violence and crime over time), a lack of human scale, shoddy construction, neglected grounds, shortcuts in the interior infrastructure (e.g., skip-stop elevators that only stopped on every other floor, a lack of lavatories on the ground floor, nonexistent recreational opportunities), and few amenities (e.g., missing baseboards, toilet seats, closet doors, or splash boards for the kitchen sink) (Bloom, 2015; Jacobs, 1961; Levenstein, 2015). Some may argue that modernism was the perfect excuse for the austerity. Examples of public housing developments included the Wendell O. Pruitt Homes and William Igoe Apartments in St. Louis, also known as Pruitt-Igoe, constructed in 1954 and torn down in 1972; the Cabrini-Green Homes, constructed between 1942 and 1962 and demolished between 1995 and 2011; and the Henry Horner Homes in Chicago, constructed between 1957 and 1963 and torn down between 1995 and 2008 (Kotlowitz, 1991). These teardowns garnered a great deal of national media attention, leading to the myth that all public housing is challenged (Bloom et al., 2015).

Over the past few decades, Congress has typically funded fewer units than authorized (Hays, 2012). While PHAs did not need to invest much in the maintenance of units during their first years as developments, they had to increase their investments over time due to price inflation (a huge concern in the 1970s and 1980s), as well as aging, wear, and tear, partially due to a very high youth ratio (Hunt, 2015). However, rents were based on residents' incomes, and PHAs' rent increases were met with resident unrest (Austen, 2018). Therefore, the Brooke Amendment, passed in 1969, capped rents at 25% of a household's income (Vale 2000). However, the Reagan Administration increased the rent cap to 30% of a household's income in the 1980s (Austen, 2018). While these caps benefitted (low-income) renters, they limited rental income for local PHAs (Moore, 2016). Over time, the discrepancy between rental revenues and costs increased, forcing Congress to vote on operating subsidies to fund the shortfall or forcing PHAs to defer investments or cut costs, resulting in deferred maintenance or minimal or nonexistent capital improvements for years or even decades (Kotlowitz, 1991).

Over the past few decades, the demographic and socioeconomic characteristics of the average residents in public housing have changed. In the 1940s, many public housing residents were non-Hispanic White, two-parent, working-class families taking advantage of low rents (Schwartz, 2021). PHAs carefully screened applicants through reference letters and home visits (Bloom & Lasner, 2016). In the 1950s and 1960s, most of these residents took advantage of FHA's mortgage insurance, the VA's Loan Guaranty Program, and FHA's Section 235, which facilitated homeownership opportunities in the suburbs, while most Black/African American public housing residents were denied these opportunities (Austen, 2018). Around the same time, some Blacks/African Americans who participated in the Great Migration moved to public housing, replacing those who bought homes in the suburbs (Von Hoffman, 2003). While many local PHAs had carefully selected renters in the 1940s and 1950s, resulting in a relatively low acceptance rate and long waitlists, they began to accept any renter in the 1960s and 1970s due to gradually increasing vacancy rates caused by an increasing number of non-Hispanic Whites moving to the suburbs (Umbach & Gerould, 2015). In the 1980s, public housing became the so-called housing of last resort, with many challenges related to poverty, violent crime, gangs, and drug dealing (Popkin, 2018). Carefully screening residents and pursuing strong eviction practices and vigorous community policing may prevent some of these challenges (Umbach & Gerould, 2015).

As of 2019, there were about 988,000 public housing units comprising 11.4% of the subsidized rental housing stock (Schwartz, 2021). Given the physical changes and funding challenges in terms of developments and the demographic and socioeconomic changes in terms of residents, most public housing developments have needed preservation, renovation, rehabilitation, recapitalization, or replacement for the past few decades. In 2019, HUD had an estimated total capital need of $70 billion, driven by investment needs for kitchens, bathrooms, heating and cooling systems, unit interiors, building exteriors, and other components (National Low Income Housing Coalition, 2019; the most recent information as of this writing).

Over the past several decades, Congress established other place-based programs, initiatives, and demonstrations, including *Homeownership for People Everywhere (HOPE) VI* from 1993 to 2010, the *Choice Neighborhoods* program since 2010, and *Rental Assistance Demonstration (RAD)* since 2013. In the *HOPE VI* program, PHAs applied to HUD in a competitive grants competition to obtain funding to demolish and redevelop developments characterized by high proportions of low-income households, high levels of crime, and funding and maintenance challenges, as well as management challenges such as high vacancy and turnover rates, physical deterioration, and a lack of support services (Bull & Gross, 2023; Goetz, 2012). As of 2010, 262 redevelopment grants totaling $6.2 billion had been awarded (Umbach & Gerould, 2015; the most recent information as of this writing). PHAs were allowed to finance redeveloped units with other public as well as private funding, achieving mixed-income housing, or to delegate redevelopment to third parties (Goetz, 2012). HOPE VI developments included rehabilitated housing, commercial investments, and revitalized neighborhoods incorporating New Urbanist design principles, which created more inviting, walkable, and safe neighborhoods that also included new jobs and improved public infrastructure (Goetz, 2012). During the first years of the program, HUD had a one-for-one replacement requirement, resulting in much criticism that first caused HUD to suspend the replacement requirement and then permanently repeal it in 1998 (Goetz, 2012). HUD encouraged PHAs to leverage private capital in 1995, before mandating it in 2002, spurring additional public and private investment and generating neighborhood spillovers (Goetz, 2012).

Many demolished units were replaced with housing choice vouchers, and about 14–25% of displaced residents returned to the

HOPE VI redevelopments after 4–8 years (Goetz, 2012). The reasons for the relatively low return rate included the lower number of redeveloped units under HOPE VI compared to the demolished public housing units, more rigid readmission standards, the relatively long time needed for redevelopment, and residents settling into their new homes and neighborhoods and trying to avoid yet another move (Goetz, 2012). On average, receiving neighborhoods had lower poverty, lower public assistance participation, and lower unemployment rates, although the rates were still high compared to the entire city (Popkin, 2018). Also, receiving neighborhoods provided little economic opportunity and few public resources (Popkin, 2018). While most displaced households reported an increased feeling of safety and thus a reduced stress level, as well as an increased level of neighborhood and housing satisfaction, they did not enjoy improvements in employment, economic security, or health and educational outcomes, all of which were the assumed outcomes of the HOPE VI program (Popkin, 2018).

Since 2010, the *Choice Neighborhoods* program has tried to address many public housing and HOPE VI concerns. It pursues a comprehensive approach that includes not only public housing but also HUD-assisted housing owned by private for-profit and nonprofit organizations, as well as the surrounding neighborhoods (Pendall et al., 2015). The program has three goals: (1) it aims to replace distressed housing with high-quality, well-managed, mixed-income housing; (2) it strives to improve employment, income, health, and educational outcomes for households in the targeted housing by offering supportive services; and (3) it lays the groundwork for public and private reinvestments that leverage the investment, leading to high-quality neighborhood assets in the target neighborhoods (Pendall et al., 2015; U.S. Department of Housing and Urban Development, n.d.k). About 60–80% of funding may be utilized for housing redevelopment and up to 15% for neighborhood projects (Pendall et al., 2015). Planning grantees may be awarded up to $500,000 for two years to prepare transformation plans, while implementation grantees may be awarded up to $30.5 million for five years (Pendall et al., 2015). As of February 2023, HUD had awarded 117 planning grants and 44 implementation grants (U.S. Department of Housing and Urban Development, 2023a).

In the *Rental Assistance Demonstration (RAD)*, based on the *Consolidated and Further Continuing Appropriations Act* of 2012, PHAs apply to HUD to transfer public housing units to the RAD program to preserve, renovate, rehabilitate, recapitalize, or replace units or developments (Stout et al., 2019; U.S. Department of Housing and Urban Development, n.d.m). As of 2020, more than 170,000 units had been converted, comprising 2.0% of the subsidized rental housing stock (Schwartz, 2021). Renters may either stay in their units, be relocated to other public housing units, be given project-based vouchers that are attached to a specific building or unit or project-based rental assistance, or be provided with HCVs that are not attached to a specific unit (U.S. Department of Housing and Urban Development, n.d.m). The RAD has partially addressed HUD's estimated total capital need of $70 billion (National Low Income Housing Coalition, 2019; the most recent information as of this writing). The most commonly used funding sources are investor equity, including tax credits, seller note/take-back financing, and commercial non-FHA loans (Stout et al., 2019). Some criticize RAD for facilitating the privatization of a large number of public housing units (Bull & Gross, 2023).

In sum, public housing has become quite diverse over time, including units in developments with few or very many units situated in detached, townhouse, semi-detached, mid-rise, or high-rise buildings located in neighborhoods that range from extreme poverty to mixed-income (Schwartz, 2021). In 2019, about 2,850 PHAs provided affordable public housing for about 985,000 households that contribute no more than 30% of their household incomes toward rent, with the government paying the remainder (Schwartz, 2021). The vast majority of households in public housing are low-income, elderly, or have members who are disabled (Popkin, 2018). Present and future challenges for HUD and the PHAs will be to maintain the aging and thus decreasingly affordable housing stock, build new units with decreasing resources, and serve eligible residents who may have chronic physical and mental health challenges, low levels of literacy and formal education, substance use, and criminal backgrounds (National Low Income Housing Coalition, 2019; Popkin, 2018).

In addition to public housing, the federal government has supported low- and moderate-income rental housing units owned by for-profit and nonprofit organizations since the Kennedy Administration (Schwartz, 2021). For example, the U.S. *Housing Act of 1961* established the Section *221(d)(3) Below Market Interest Rate (BMIR)* program, in which private lenders originated mortgages with a typical interest rate of around 3%, compared to a market rate of around 6.5%, and then sold these mortgages to Fannie Mae at market rate, with the FHA subsidizing and insuring the difference. This ultimately led to moderate-income rental housing units with rents that would otherwise have been impossible to obtain (Anonymous, 1995). Beneficiaries were households that had household incomes slightly above the eligibility threshold for public housing but were unable or unwilling to pursue homeownership (Hays, 2012). From 1961 to 1968, Section 221(d)(3) BMIR produced 184,000 units in total (Schwartz, 2021). The program was terminated in 1968, as some critics argued that it served moderate-income (and thus undeserving) renters who were able to afford relatively high rents and that the program was financially unsustainable (Schwartz, 2021).

The *Housing and Urban Development Act of 1968* established the Section 236 program, which replaced the Section 221(d)(3) BMIR program and the rent supplements for eligible low-income renters that ran from 1965 to 1973 (Landis, 2012). Section 236 subsidized lenders that collaborated with cooperatives, nonprofit organizations, or limited dividend, for-profit organizations that constructed or rehabilitated rent-restricted multifamily rental and cooperative housing (Silver, 2012). These sponsors took out mortgages at market rate (about 7%) but only paid 1% interest on mortgages, with the remainder subsidized and insured by the FHA (Silver, 2012). Section 236 produced more than 544,000 units before being terminated in 1973 (Weicher, 2012). As of 2020, approximately 26,000 units still remained in the Section 236 and Section 221(d)(3) programs, comprising 0.3% of the subsidized rental housing stock (Schwartz, 2021).

President Nixon declared a moratorium on housing and community development assistance in 1973, including funding for public housing, such as Urban Renewal and Model Cities programs and Sections 235 and 236, due to criticisms that most newly established major programs had been failures. Instead, he called for a completely new approach to assistance (Hays, 2012). Thus, the Section 8 project-based rental assistance programs replaced the Section 236 program in 1974 (Popkin, 2018). HUD established the Section 8 *New Construction Substantial Rehabilitation (NC/SR)* program, which provided a direct rental subsidy for eligible low-income renters by paying housing providers the difference between the Fair Market Rent (FMR), determined by HUD, and 25% (later 30%) of the household's income (Weicher, 2012). The Section 8 NC/SR program produced more than 850,000 units and was terminated in 1983, as critics pointed out relatively high development and operating costs due to relatively high FMRs and interest rates and mandated social services, all leading to relatively high rents (NYU Furman Center, 2018a, 2018b). As of 2020, the Section 8 NC/SR program still had almost 560,000 units, comprising 6.5% of the subsidized rental housing stock (Schwartz, 2021).

Congress passed the *CDBG Program* in 1974, which consolidated several categorical grant programs to be more cost effective (Anonymous, 1995; Bull & Gross, 2023). As of Fiscal Year (FY) 2023, $3.33 billion had been enacted for this program (U.S. Department of Housing and Urban Development, n.d.a; n.d.l.). The goal of the program is to develop decent housing and suitable living environments and to expand economic opportunities for primarily low- and moderate-income persons by acquiring, rehabilitating, relocating, and demolishing residential and nonresidential properties, constructing and improving public facilities and public services (such as water and sewer facilities, streets, and neighborhood centers, among others), and investing in economic development and job creation and retention activities (U.S. Department of Housing and Urban Development, n.d.c). Eligible grantees are principal cities of Metropolitan Statistical Areas (MSAs), other cities in metropolitan areas with populations of at least 50,000, and qualified urban counties with populations of at least 200,000 (excluding the population of entitled cities; U.S. Department of Housing and Urban Development, n.d.c). These eligible grantees must spend more than 70% of the allotted CDBG funds on activities that benefit low- and moderate-income persons (U.S. Department of Housing and Urban Development, n.d.c).

In 1986, Congress established the *LIHTC* program, which is administered by the U.S. Treasury and has annually financed the vast majority of all income-restricted affordable rental housing, resulting in almost 2.77 million below-market rate units as of 2018 (Cadik, n.d.; Schwartz, 2021; U.S. Department of Housing and Urban Development, 2018; the most recent information as of this writing). The program has the goal of incentivizing investments by developers who build and rehabilitate rental housing that is affordable to eligible low- and moderate-income households for at least 30 years (U.S. Department of Housing and Urban Development, 2018). Most rents are set so that households at exactly 60% of AMI do not pay more than 30% of their income, but most households with incomes below 60% pay more (K. McClure, personal email to author, April 2, 2020; Williamson, 2011).

In the early years of the LIHTC program, funding was typically combined with resources from other programs and sources, such as the federal HOME Investment Partnerships Program, the CDBG program, the National Housing Trust fund, and state housing trust funds (Scally, Anoli, et al., 2018). Recently, layered subsidy has become less common (K. McClure, personal email to author, April 2, 2020). Partners in an LIHTC deal are federal, state, and local government agencies, equity investors, attorneys, and project developers or owners, along with housing funds (Scally, Anoli, et al., 2018).

LIHTC investors claim tax credits over a ten-year period and need to comply over a 15-year period, discounting the future value of a projected income stream (Bull & Gross, 2023; Scally, Anoli, et al., 2018). There are two tax credits that determine the financing for each project. The first is the highly competitive *9% tax credit*, set at 70% of the present value of the initial development costs, excluding the cost of land and certain other expenses. This tax credit is allocated annually by the Internal Revenue Service (IRS) to state housing finance agencies (HFAs) so they can award tax credits to developers that either reduce their federal income tax by $1 for every dollar of tax credit received or sell the tax credit to investors to raise funds for the development costs of projects (Shanholtz, 2016). States will either receive at least $3,105,000 or $2.70 per capita, whichever is higher (Scally, Anoli, et al., 2018).

The success of an application for the 9% tax credit is determined by its respective state's annually updated Qualified Allocation Plan (QAP), which has scoring criteria based on established priorities such as: (1) minimum affordability periods; (2) preservation projects; (3) a location in a low-income neighborhood; (4) projects providing services to residents; (5) access to services such as jobs, public schools, and transportation; and (6) bonus points for meeting sustainable green building standards (Scally, Anoli, et al., 2018). LIHTC projects may obtain bonus tax credits when they are built in Qualified

Census Tracts (QCTs), now defined as tracts that have 50% of households with incomes below 60% of the Area Median Gross Income (AMGI) or have a poverty rate of 25% or more, based on the Consolidated Appropriations Act of 2018 (U.S. Department of Housing and Urban Development, 2018, n.d.c). The second tax credit is a non-competitive *4% tax credit* that is bundled with the tax-exempt government bonds (Kawitzky et al., 2013). In other words, the tax credits and the bonds provide the subsidy.

Developers who apply for the latter uncapped tax credit typically directly apply at the IRS and do not go through their respective states (Scally, Anoli, et al., 2018). However, developers may have to apply competitively for the tax-exempt bonds in combination with the 4% credits in some jurisdictions. The LIHTC program is funded by the Internal Revenue Service (IRS), which awards tax credits to state housing finance agencies that have considerable flexibility in administering the LIHTC program (Deng, 2007). While some states prefer large, clustered developments, others prefer small, dispersed ones (Deng, 2007). Some states may focus on expanding the affordable housing supply in opportunity neighborhoods, whereas others may focus on challenged neighborhoods (Deng, 2007).

In the past, present, and near future, place-based programs have faced and will continue to face preservation challenges (Schwartz, 2021). In terms of housing affordability challenges, many units have converted or will convert to market-rate housing, which may be unaffordable to current renters (Schwartz, 2021). Also, some owners face deferred maintenance issues, which may be difficult to address because rent increases must be approved by HUD, possibly preventing building a reserve fund for capital investments (Schwartz, 2021).

10.2 PEOPLE-BASED PROGRAMS

In terms of people-based programs, there is the Section 8 *Voucher/Housing Choice Voucher (HCV) Program*, funded by HUD. As of 2019, there were almost 2.6 million households living in housing units supported by an HCV, which comprised about 29.5% of the subsidized rental housing stock (Schwartz, 2021). The program's primary goal is to assist eligible low-income households containing U.S. citizens or non-citizens with an eligible immigration status and who earn less than 50% of the AMI of the metropolitan area or county in selecting and paying for moderately priced, decent, safe, and sanitary rental market-rate housing (U.S. Department of Housing and Urban Development, n.d.d). However, the program requires that at least 75% of HCVs are allocated to households with incomes below 30% of the AMI. The secondary goal of the program is to reduce residential racial and ethnic segregation and poverty concentration in neighborhoods (Goetz, 2013).

Program participants are both households and housing providers. Households receive a housing choice voucher to look for affordable housing on the private market, or they may join the waitlist of a local public housing agency (PHA), as demand typically exceeds the capped supply (U.S. Department of Housing and Urban Development, n.d.d). PHAs may establish preferences for waitlisted households, prioritizing homeless households, households living in substandard housing, households spending more than 50% of their income for rent, and involuntarily displaced households (U.S. Department of Housing and Urban Development, n.d.d).

Housing providers rent out housing units that meet the minimum standards of health and safety, do not surpass maximum standards such as the number of bedrooms, and can be inspected by the respective local PHA (Lopez, 2012; U.S. Department of Housing and Urban Development, n.d.d). Housing units may be apartments, townhouses, or single-family homes on the private market or units in public housing (U.S. Department of Housing and Urban Development, n.d.d).

The amount of a housing choice voucher depends on a household's income, assets, and number of members and is determined by the respective local PHA (U.S. Department of Housing and Urban Development, n.d.d). However, a voucher household must pay 30% but cannot pay more than 40% of its monthly adjusted gross income (AGI) for rent and utilities (U.S. Department of Housing and Urban Development, n.d.d). The housing choice voucher is funded by HUD, is awarded and administered by the PHA that transfers the subsidy to the participating housing provider, and is valid for at least 60 days (U.S. Department of Housing and Urban Development, n.d.d).

At the national level, only about 25% of households eligible for vouchers receive them (Gramlich, 2022). About 69% of vouchers issued to households resulted in an actual lease and assistance contract with a housing provider in 2000 (Center on Budget and Policy

Priorities, 2019; the most recent information as of this writing). Market and individual factors may determine the voucher success rate. In terms of the former, the success rate may be determined by the presence or absence of market tightness, antidiscrimination laws, and the level of the payment standard relative to the FMR (Schwartz, 2021; U.S. Department of Housing and Urban Development, n.d.f). In terms of the latter, the rate may be determined by race, ethnicity, and the age and gender of the head of the household (Schwartz, 2021).

In 1992, the U.S. Department of Housing and Urban Development began the ten-year-long *Moving to Opportunity for Fair Housing Demonstration (MTO)* program in five participating cities: Baltimore, Boston, Chicago, Los Angeles, and New York. It spent about $80 million, giving two groups of public housing residents in each city an HCV but constraining one group in its location choices to neighborhoods with less than 10% poverty (treatment group 1) and not constraining the other group in their location choices (treatment group 2), while also having a group remain in public housing (control group) (Greenlee, 2020). The MTO demonstration was motivated by a desire to help HCV households make better use of the mobility provided by the HCV program by moving to neighborhoods offering higher levels of opportunity (McClure, 2020). While movers in treatment group 1 achieved gains in mental and physical health, subjective well-being, and family safety, they did not have improvements in education and labor market outcomes and, thus, household incomes in the short run (Sanbonmatsu et al., 2011). However, moving to a lower-poverty neighborhood before age 13 increases college attendance and earnings and reduces single parenthood rates, whereas moving to a lower-poverty neighborhood after age 13 has some negative outcomes in the long run, perhaps due to disruption (Chetty et al., 2016).

In sum, both place-based and people-based programs have faced challenges in terms of funding, the aging and thus decreasing affordable housing stock, complicated program designs, extensive application and implementation requirements and processes, and clients with multiple challenges. In the near and distant future, traditional public housing will become a phenomenon of the past. Recent and future public housing will be public-private partnerships, and private housing will be part of place-based programs (through the Section 8 NC/SR or LIHTC programs) or people-based programs (through the HCV programs). Thus, the focus on philanthropy in housing will increase, a topic that has not been much discussed in planning.

SUMMARY OF PART II

- The U.S. housing policy landscape is balkanized into dozens of programs, demonstrations, and initiatives.
- Homeownership policy is primarily supported by tax policy and rentership policy is supported by tax expenditures.
- Housing policy is typically reactive instead of proactive.
- The New Deal established many current public and semipublic housing institutions, policies, and programs, most of them still operating today.
- In the 1960s and 1970s, Congress addressed racial and ethnic housing and credit discrimination.
- The Great Recession of 2007 to 2009 was a watershed moment in urban housing policy and owner-occupied housing.
- Homeownership has been facilitated by tax policy through deductions, exemptions, and tax credits for more than a century.
- Policies have attempted to address the overall nationwide shortage of habitable and affordable housing and moderate-income homeownership. One example is the FHA, which designed the 20- to 30-year, standardized, low down payment, low-interest, fixed-rate, amortizing mortgage for single-family homes. Another example is the secondary mortgage market, which provides finances for the housing market.
- Several place-based and people-based policies and programs, primarily administered by HUD, benefit low- and moderate-income renters.

DOI: 10.1201/9781032657646-14

APPENDIX

Overview of Select Housing Legislation and Organizations, 1932 Until Present

Years	Housing legislation	Housing organizations and programs
1930s		
1932	Federal Home Loan Bank Act	Reconstruction Finance Corporation created
		Federal Home Loan Bank Board and Bank System created
1933	National Industrial Recovery Act Homeowners' Loan Act	Housing Division of Public Works Administration (PWA) created
		Homeowners Loan Corporation (HOLC) formed
1934	National Housing Act	Federal Housing Administration (FHA) created
1937	U.S. Housing Act of 1937	United States Housing Authority (USHA) established (superseded by Housing and Home Finance Agency [1947–1965] and U.S. Department of Housing and Urban Development [1965 to present])
1938		Fannie Mae (FNMA) chartered
1940s		
1942	Executive Order 9070	National Housing Agency formed (consolidated FHA, FHLBB, HOLC, and USHA, among many others)

(Continued)

(Continued)

Years	Housing legislation	Housing organizations and programs
1944	Servicemen's Readjustment Act (GI Bill)	
1947	Reorganization Plan Number 3	Housing and Home Finance Agency formed (superseded by U.S. Department of Housing and Urban Development [1965 to present])
1949	U.S. Housing Act of 1949	Slum Clearance and *Community Development* program established
1950s		
1954	U.S. Housing Act of 1954	Slum Clearance and *Urban Redevelopment* program created
1960s		
1961	U.S. Housing Act of 1961	Section 221(d)(3) authorized
1964	Civil Rights Act of 1964	
1965	Department of Housing and Urban Development Act of 1965	U.S. Department of Housing and Urban Development (HUD) created
	Voting Rights Act of 1965	
1966	Demonstration Cities and Metropolitan Development Act of 1966	Model Cities program Rent supplement
	Model Cities Act	
1968	Housing and Urban Development Act of 1968	Fannie Mae privatized Government National Mortgage Association (GNMA) created
	1968 Fair Housing Act	Section 235 program created Section 236 program created
1969	Brooke Amendment (25% of income)	
1970s		
1970	Housing and Urban Development Act of 1970	Freddie Mac created Community Development Corporations (CDCs) established
	Emergency Home Finance Act	
1973	Rehabilitation Act of 1973	Nixon Moratorium on HUD Programs

(Continued)

Years	Housing legislation	Housing organizations and programs
1974	Housing and Community Development Act of 1974	Community Development Block Grants (CDBGs) consolidate categorical grant programs Section 8 Rental Assistance established (project-based and tenant-based)
1975	Home Mortgage Disclosure Act (HMDA)	
1980s		
1980	Depository Institutions' Deregulation and Monetary Control Act of 1980	
1981	Brooke Amendment (30% of income)	
1983	Housing and Urban Recovery Act	
1984		Section 8 Voucher Demonstration
1986	Tax Reform Act of 1986	Low Income Housing Tax Credit (LIHTC) established
1987	McKinney Act	Section 8 Voucher Program
1989	Fair Housing Amendments Act 1989 HUD Reform Act	
1990s		
1990	1990 National Affordable Housing Act (Cranston-Gonzalez) Low Income Housing Preservation and Residential Homeownership Act of 1990 Americans with Disabilities Act of 1990	HOME Program passed
1992	1992 Housing Community Development Act	Office of Federal Housing Enterprise Oversight (OFHEO) created (superseded by Federal Housing Finance Agency, 2008 to present)

(Continued)

Years	Housing legislation	Housing organizations and programs
1993	Government Performance and Results Act of 1993	HOPE VI Program
1996	Native American Housing Assistance and Self Determination Act of 1996	
2000s		
2000	American Homeownership and Economic Opportunity Act of 2000	
	Community Renewal Tax Relief Act of 2000	
2008	Housing and Economic Recovery Act of 2008	Federal Housing Finance Agency (FHFA) created
		Fannie Mae and Freddie Mac placed into conservatorship
		Housing Trust Fund authorized
2009	American Recovery and Reinvestment Act (ARRA) HEARTH Act of 2009	Neighborhood Stabilization Programs (NSPs)
2010s		
2010	Dodd-Frank Wall Street Reform and Consumer Protection Act of 2010	Choice Neighborhoods Program
2013		Rental Assistance Demonstration (RAD)
2014		Promise Zones

Sources: author, based on Anonymous, 1995; Hays, 2012; McClure, 2018; U.S. Department of Housing and Urban Development, n.d.a, n.d.b, n.d.c, n.d.d, n.d.e, n.d.f , n.d.g, n.d.h, n.d.i, n.d.j; Vale, 2000.

REFERENCES

Abel, J., & Fuster, A. (2021). How do mortgage refinances affect debt, default, and spending? Evidence from HARP. *American Economic Journal: Macroeconomics, 13*(2), 254–291.

Abramsky, S. (2013). *The American way of poverty: How the other half still lives.* Nation Books.

Adams, C. T. (2014). *From the outside in: Suburban elites, third-sector organizations, and the reshaping of Philadelphia.* Cornell University Press.

Aktas, C. B., & Bilec, M. M. (2012). Impact of lifetime on U.S. residential building: LCA results. *The International Journal of Life Cycle Assessment, 17*(3), 337–349.

Alexander, M. (2012). *The new Jim Crow: Mass incarceration in the age of colorblindness.* The New Press.

Alexandrov, A., Goodman, L., & Tozer, T. (2022, August). *Normalizing forbearance.* https://www.urban.org/research/publication/normalizing-forbearance

Ali, S. H., Connolly, C., & Keil, R. (2023). *Pandemic urbanism: Infectious diseases on a planet of cities.* Polity.

Allen, J. G., & Macomber, J. D. (2020). *Healthy buildings: How indoor spaces drive performance and productivity.* Harvard University Press.

Allon, F. (2008). *Renovation nation: Our obsession with home.* University of New South Wales Press.

Alvarez, T., & Steffen, B. L. (2021). *Worst case housing needs: 2021 report to Congress.* https://www.huduser.gov/portal/sites/default/files/pdf/Worst-Case-Housing-Needs-2021.pdf

American Cancer Society (n.d.). *Radon and cancer.* https://www.cancer.org/cancer/cancer-causes/radiation-exposure/radon.html

American Civil Liberties Union (n.d.). *FAQs: United Nations Special Rapporteurs.* https://www.aclu.org/other/faqs-united-nations-special-rapporteurs

American Farmland Trust (2016). *Cost of community services studies.* https://s30428.pcdn.co/wp-content/uploads/sites/2/2019/09/Cost_of_Community_Services_Studies_AFT_FIC_201609.pdf

Anacker, K. B. (2015a). The little downpayment savings policy that could: Revisiting building and loan societies and their products in times of the tight credit box and the pending housing finance reform. *Housing and Society, 42*(2), 101–113.

Anacker, K. B. (2015b). Analyzing census tract foreclosure risk rates in mature and developing suburbs in the United States. *Urban Geography, 36*(8), 1221–1240.

Anacker, K. B. (Ed.). (2015c). *The new American suburb: Poverty, race and the economic crisis.* Routledge.

Anacker, K. B. (2018). The Great Recession. In K. B. Anacker, A. T. Carswell, S. D. Kirby, & K. R. Tremblay (Eds.), *Introduction to housing* (pp. 255–272). University of Georgia Press.

Anacker, K. B. (2019). Introduction: Housing affordability and affordable housing. *International Journal of Housing Policy, 19*(1), 1–16.

Anacker, K. B. (2020). Inclusionary zoning and inclusionary housing in the United States: Measuring inputs and outcomes. In R. Philips, E. Trevan, & P. Kraeger (Eds.), *Research handbook on community development* (pp. 189–203). Edward Elgar.

Anacker, K. B. (2022). U.S. suburbs and the global COVID-19 pandemic: From cleanscapes to safescapes? The case of the New York metropolitan area. *Urban Geography, 43*(8), 1260–1267.

Anacker, K. B., Carswell, A. T., Kirby, S. D., & Tremblay, K. R. (Eds.). (2018). *Introduction to housing.* University of Georgia Press.

Anacker, K. B., & Crossney, K. B. (2013). Analyzing CRA lending during the tsunami in subprime lending and foreclosure in the Philadelphia MSA. *Housing Studies, 28*(4), 529–552.

Anacker, K. B., & Li, Y. (2016). Analyzing housing affordability of U.S. renters during the Great Recession, 2007 to 2009. *Housing and Society, 43*(1), 1–17.

Anacker, K. B., & Niedt, C. (2023). Classifying regulatory approaches of jurisdictions for Accessory Dwelling Units: The case of Long Island. *Journal of Planning Education and Research, 43*(1), 60–80.

Anacker, K. B., Niedt, C., & Kwon, C. (2017). Analyzing segregation in mature and developing suburbs in the United States. *Journal of Urban Affairs, 39*(6), 819–832.

Angell, C., & Patel, K. (2017). Origins of the crisis. In F. Carns (Ed.), *Crisis and response: An FDIC history, 2008–2013* (pp. 1–32). Federal Deposit Insurance Corporation.

Anonymous (n.d.). *U.S. Government manual: Federal Deposit Insurance Corporation.* Government Printing Office.

Anonymous (1995). 63 Years of federal action in housing and urban development. *Cityscape, 3*(1), vi–ix.

Anonymous (2010a). *The 2007–2009 Recession: Similarities to and differences from the past.* https://fas.org/sgp/crs/misc/R40198.pdf

Anonymous (2010b, December 24). NSP at halftime. *Shelterforce.*

Anonymous (2016, June 27). *Mortality in the United States: Past, present, and future.* University of Pennsylvania Wharton School. https://budgetmodel. wharton.upenn.edu/issues/2016/1/25/mortality-in-the-united-states-past-present-and-future

Aragão, C. (2023, March 1). *Gender pay gap in U.S. hasn't changed much in two decades.* https://www.pewresearch.org/short-reads/2023/03/01/gender-pay-gap-facts/

Arias, E., Tejada-Vera, B., Ahmad, F., & Kochanek, K. D. (2021). *Provisional life expectancy estimates for 2020.* https://www.cdc.gov/nchs/data/vsrr/vsrr015-508.pdf

Asante-Muhammed, D., Collins, C., Hoxie, J., & Nieves, E. (2016). *The ever-growing gap: Without change, African-American [sic] and Latino families won't match White wealth for centuries.* https://ips-dc.org/report-ever-growing-gap/

Associated Press (2020, December 21). *Highlights of $900 billion COVID-19 relief, wrapup bills.* https://apnews.com/article/health-care-reform-health-legislation-coronavirus-pandemic-762f84e4da11d350d8b5be5680ab01c4

Attom Data Solutions (2019, January 15). U.S. foreclosure activity drops to 13-year low in 2018. https://www.attomdata.com/news/most-recent/2018-year-end-foreclosure-market-report/

Aurand, A., Pish, M., Rafi, I., & Yentel, D. (2023). *Out of reach: The high cost of housing.* https://nlihc.org/oor

Austen, B. (2018). *High-risers: Cabrini-Green and the fate of American public housing.* Harper.

Bachaud, N. (2021, July 8). It's harder to save for a downpayment, but today's first-time buyers have some unique opportunities. https://www.zillow.com/research/how-long-to-save-a-down-payment-29735/

Baily, M. N. (2011). Preface. In M. N. Baily (Ed.), *The future of housing finance: Restructuring the U.S. residential mortgage market* (pp. vii–x). Brookings Institution Press.

Balsam, J., & Gorman, K. (2023, March 2). *Decreased competition from home ownership in increasing interest rate environment.* https://www.novoco.com/periodicals/articles/decreased-competition-home-ownership-increasing-interest-rate-environment

Baradaran, M. (2015). *How the other half banks: Exclusion, exploitation, and the threat to democracy.* Harvard University Press.

Barone, E. (2020, December 21). *How the new COVID-19 pandemic relief bill stacks up to other countries' economic responses.* https://time.com/5923840/us-pandemic-relief-bill-december/

Barth, J. R. (2009). *The rise and fall of the U.S. mortgage and credit markets: A comprehensive analysis of the market meltdown.* John Wiley & Sons, Inc.

Bartram, R. (2022). *Stacked decks: Building inspectors and the reproduction of urban inequality.* The University of Chicago Press.

Baxandall, R., & Ewen, E. (2000). *Picture windows: How the suburbs happened.* Basic Books.

Beamish, J. O., & Goss, R. C. (2018). Influences on housing choice. In K. B. Anacker, A. T. Carswell, S. D. Kirby, & K. R. Tremblay (Eds.), *Introduction to housing* (pp. 21–39). University of Georgia Press.

Benson, S. P. (2007). *Household accounts: Working-class family economies in the interwar United States.* Cornell University Press.

Berg, B. F. (2018). *New York City politics: Governing Gotham.* Rutgers University Press.

Bernanke, B. S. (2015). *The courage to act: A memoir of a crisis and its aftermath.* W. W. Norton & Company.

Bernanke, B. S. (2022). *21st century monetary policy: The Federal Reserve from the great inflation to COVID-19.* W. W. Norton.

Bernanke, B. S., Geithner, T. F., Paulson, H. M., & Ling, N. (Eds.). (2020). *First responders: Inside the U.S. strategy for fighting the 2007–2009 Global Financial Crisis.* Yale University Press.

Berry, K. (2023, March 8). Silvergate Bank says it's self-liquidating, winding down operations. https://www.nationalmortgagenews.com/news/silvergate-bank-say-its-self-liquidating-winding-down-operations

Betancur, J. J., & Smith, J. L. (2016). *Claiming neighborhood: New ways of understanding urban change.* University of Illinois Press.

Bhutta, N., Chang, A. C., Dettling, L. J., & Hsu, J. W. (2020, September 28). *Disparities in wealth by race and ethnicity in the 2019 Survey of Consumer Finances.* https://www.federalreserve.gov/econres/notes/feds-notes/disparities-in-wealth-by-race-and-ethnicity-in-the-2019-survey-of-consumer-finances-20200928.html

Bhutta, N., & Ringo, D. (2016, September 29). *Changing FHA mortgage insurance premiums and the effects on lending* (FEDS Notes). https://www.federalreserve.gov/econresdat/notes/feds-notes/2016/changing-fha-mortgage-insurance-premiums-and-the-effects-on-lending-20160929.html

Bivens, J. (2019, April 2018). *What should we know about the next recession?* https://www.epi.org/publication/next-recession-bivens/

Black, A. N. D., & Robinson, J. B. (1959). Statement of Algernon D. Black, Chairman, New York State Committee on Discrimination in Housing and Acting Chairman of the National Committee against Discrimination in Housing, accompanied by Joseph B. Robison, Chairman of the Legal Committee, New York State Committee on Discrimination in Housing and Director, Commission on Law and Social Action, American Jewish Congress. In *Hearings before the United States Commission on Civil Rights: Housing.* Government Printing Office.

Blinder, A. S. (2014). *After the music stopped: The financial crisis, the response, and the work ahead.* Penguin Books.

Bloom, N. D. (2008). *Public housing that worked: New York in the twentieth century*. University of Pennsylvania Press.

Bloom, N. D. (2015). Myth #4: High-rise public housing is unmanageable. In N. D. Bloom, F. Umbach, & L. J. Vale (Eds.), *Public housing myths: Perception, reality, and social policy* (pp. 91–118). Cornell University Press.

Bloom, N. D., & Lasner, M. G. (2016). Introduction. In N. D. Bloom & M. G. Lasner (Eds.), *Affordable housing in New York: The people, the places, and policies that transformed a city* (pp. 1–14). Columbia University Press.

Bloom, N. D., Umbach, F., & Vale, L. J. (Eds.). (2015). Introduction. In N. D. Bloom, F. Umbach, & L. J. Vale (Eds.), *Public housing myths: Perception, reality, and social policy* (pp. 1–28). Cornell University Press.

Bodfish, H. M. (Ed.). (1931). *History of building and loan in the United States*. United States Building and Loan League.

Botein, H., & Hetling, A. (2016). *Home safe home: Housing solutions for survivors of intimate partner violence*. Rutgers University Press.

Bourassa, S. C., & Grigsby, W. G. (2000). Income tax concessions for owner-occupied housing. *Housing Policy Debate, 11*(3), 521–546.

Boushey, H., Nunn, R., O'Donnell, J., & Shambaugh, J. (2019). The damage done by recessions and how to respond. In H. Boushey, R. Nunn, & J. Shambaugh (Eds.), *Recession ready: Fiscal policies to stabilize the American economy* (pp. 11–47). The Brookings Institution Press.

Boushey, H., & Shambaugh, J. (2019). Introduction. In H. Boushey, R. Nunn, & J. Shambaugh (Eds.), *Recession ready: Fiscal policies to stabilize the American economy* (pp. 5–9). The Brookings Institution Press.

Bradford, C., & Shlay, A. B. (1996). Assuming a can opener: Economic theory's failure to explain discrimination in FHA lending markets. *Cityscape, 2*(1), 77–87.

Brandlee, K. (2011). *Promoting homeownership in the United States: The rise and fall of Fannie Mae and Freddie Mac*. University of Iowa Center for International Finance and Development.

Bratt, R. G. (2012). Public housing. In A. T. Carswell (Ed.), *The encyclopedia of housing* (pp. 569–574). SAGE.

Bratt, R. G. (2020). The U.S. approach to social housing. In K. B. Anacker, M. T. Nguyen, & D. P. Varady (Eds.), *The Routledge handbook of housing policy and planning* (pp. 173–188). Routledge.

Bratt, R. G., Stone, M. E., & Hartman, C. (Eds.). (2006). *A right to housing: Foundation for a new social agenda*. Temple University Press.

Bremen, J. M. (2023, May 17). Why salary increases *still* do not align with inflation. https://www.forbes.com/sites/johnbremen/2023/05/17/why-salary-increases-still-do-not-align-with-inflation/?sh=2e64be9e5d0d

Brevoort, K. P., Grimm, P., & Kambara, M. (2015). *Data point: Credit invisibles*. https://files.consumerfinance.gov/f/201505_cfpb_data-point-credit-invisibles.pdf

Brown, P. H. (2015). *How real estate developers think: Design, profits, and community*. University of Pennsylvania Press.

Bruin, M. J., & Mitchell, D. (2018). Home buying and homeownership. In K. B. Anacker, A. T. Carswell, S. D. Kirby, & K. R. Tremblay (Eds.), *Introduction to housing* (pp. 121–138). University of Georgia Press.

Bull, M., & Gross, A. (2023). *Housing in America: An introduction*. Routledge.

Bureau of Economic Analysis (2023, January 26). *Gross Domestic Product, fourth quarter and year 2022 (advance estimate)*. https://www.bea.gov/news/2023/gross-domestic-product-fourth-quarter-and-year-2022-advance-estimate#:~:text=Current%2Ddollar%20GDP%20increased%209.2,(tables%201%20and%203).

Bureau of Labor Statistics (n.d.a). *Labor force statistics from the Current Population Survey*. https://www.bls.gov/cps/

Bureau of Labor Statistics (n.d.b). *How the Government measures unemployment*. https://www.bls.gov/cps/cps_htgm.htm

Burns, J., & Porter, C. (2016). *Big shifts ahead: Demographic clarity for businesses*. Advantage.

Cadik, E. (n.d.). *The Low-Income Housing Tax Credit*. https://www.enterprisecommunity.org/policy-and-advocacy/policy-priorities/low-income-housing-tax-credits

Calabria, M. (2011, May 7). *Fannie, Freddie, and the subprime mortgage market*. https://www.cato.org/publications/briefing-paper/fannie-freddie-subprime-mortgage-market

Camarota, S. A., & Zeigler, K. (2022, October 27). *Foreign-born population hits nearly 48 million in September 2022: An increase of 2.9 million since the start of the Biden administration*. https://cis.org/Report/ForeignBorn-Populatio-n-Hits-Nearly-48-Million-September-2022

Carns, F. (2017). Overview. In F. Carns (Ed.), *Crisis and response: An FDIC history, 2008–2013* (pp. xi–xl). Federal Deposit Insurance Corporation.

Carter, B., & McGoldrick, M. (1989). *The changing family life cycle*. Allyn and Bacon.

Case, A., & Deaton, A. (2021). *Deaths of despair and the future of capitalism*. Princeton University Press.

Caves, R. W. (2012a). Housing Act of 1949. In A. T. Carswell (Ed.), *The encyclopedia of housing* (pp. 333–334). SAGE.

Caves, R. W. (2012b). Housing Act of 1954. In A. T. Carswell (Ed.), *The encyclopedia of housing* (pp. 334–335). SAGE.

Caves, R. W. (2012c). Housing and Urban Development Act of 1968. In A. T. Carswell (Ed.), *The encyclopedia of housing* (pp. 338–339). SAGE.

Center for Neighborhood Technology (n.d.). Housing and Transportation (H+T®) Affordability Index. https://cnt.org/tools/housing-and-transportation-affordability-index

Center on Budget and Policy Priorities (2019, March 4). *Housing voucher success and utilization indicators, and understanding utilization data*. https://www.cbpp.

org/research/housing/housing-voucher-success-and-utilization-indicators-and-understanding-utilization

Center on Budget and Policy Priorities (2023, June 13). *Chart book: Tracking the recovery from the pandemic recession.* https://www.cbpp.org/research/economy/tracking-the-recovery-from-the-pandemic-recession#pandemic_recession_deeper

Centers for Disease Control and Prevention (n.d.a). *Home and recreational safety: Older adult falls: Important facts about falls.* https://www.cdc.gov/homeandrecreationalsafety/falls/index.html

Centers for Disease Control and Prevention (n.d.b). *Home and recreational safety: Poisoning.* https://www.cdc.gov/homeandrecreationalsafety/poisoning/index.html

Centers for Disease Control and Prevention (n.d.c). *What you should know about COVID-19 to protect yourself and others.* https://www.cdc.gov/coronavirus/2019-ncov/prevent-getting-sick/prevention.html

Centers for Disease Control and Prevention (n.d.d). *Provisional death counts for Coronavirus Disease (COVID-19).* https://www.cdc.gov/nchs/nvss/vsrr/covid19/index.htm

Centers for Disease Control and Prevention (n.d.e). *Table BRTH: Crude birth rates, fertility rates, and birth rates by age, race, and Hispanic origin of mother: United States, selected years 1950–2019.* https://www.cdc.gov/nchs/data/hus/2020-2021/Brth.pdf

Centers for Disease Control and Prevention (2017). Table 15: *Life expectancy at birth, at age 65, and at age 75, by sex, race, and Hispanic origin: United States, selected years 1900–2016.* https://www.cdc.gov/nchs/data/hus/2017/015.pdf

Centers for Medicare and Medicaid Services (n.d.). NHE fact sheet. https://www.cms.gov/research-statistics-data-and-systems/statistics-trends-and-reports/nationalhealthexpenddata/nhe-fact-sheet

Chappell, B. (2022, April 28). Here's why Dr. Fauci says the U.S. is 'out of the pandemic phase'. https://www.npr.org/2022/04/27/1094997608/fauci-us-pandemic-phase-covid-19

Chatterjee, L., Harvey, D., & Klugman, L. (1974). *FHA policies and the Baltimore City housing market.* Johns Hopkins University Press.

Chetty, R., Hendren, N., & Katz, L. F. (2016). The effects of exposure to better neighborhoods on children: New evidence from the moving to opportunity experiment. *American Economic Review, 106*(4), 855–902.

Clements, M. (2023, April). *Bank regulation: Preliminary review of agency actions related to March 2023 bank failures. Report to the Committee on Financial Services, House of Representatives.* https://www.gao.gov/assets/gao-23-106736.pdf

Coates, T.-N. (2017). *We were eight years in power: An American tragedy.* One World.

Cochrane, E. (2021, March 6). Divided Senate passes Biden's pandemic aid plan. *The New York Times.*

Cohen, J. N. (2017). *Financial crisis in American households: The basic expenses that bankrupt the middle class.* Praeger.

Cohn, D'V., Horowitz, J. M., Minkin, R., Fry, R., & Hurst, K. (2022). *1. The demographics of multigenerational households.* https://www.pewresearch.org/social-trends/2022/03/24/the-demographics-of-multigenerational-households/

Colburn, G., & Aldern, C. P. (2022). *Homelessness is a housing problem: How structural factors explain U.S. patterns.* University of California Press.

Collins v. Mnuchin, 17–20364 U.S. Court of Appeals for the Fifth Circuit (New Orleans).

Colton, K. W. (2003). *Housing in the twenty-first century: Achieving common ground.* Harvard University Press.

Committee on Small Business (2019, June 20). *Hearing: The importance of accurate Census data to small business formation and growth.* https://docs.house.gov/Committee/Calendar/ByEvent.aspx?EventID=109662

Commonwealth of Virginia (2020, March 30). *Executive Order 55: Temporary stay at home order due to novel Coronavirus (COVID-19).* https://www.governor.virginia.gov/media/governorvirginiagov/executive-actions/EO-55-Temporary-Stay-at-Home-Order-Due-to-Novel-Coronavirus-(COVID-19).pdf

Congressional Budget Office (1991). *Controlling the risks of Government-Sponsored Enterprises.* https://www.cbo.gov/publication/19583

Consumer Financial Protection Bureau (n.d.). *Learn about forbearance.* https://www.consumerfinance.gov/coronavirus/mortgage-and-housing-assistance/help-for-homeowners/learn-about-forbearance/

Consumer Financial Protection Bureau (2023, June 29). *Summary of 2022 data on mortgage lending.* https://www.consumerfinance.gov/data-research/hmda/summary-of-2022-data-on-mortgage-lending/#:~:text=The%202022%20data%20include%20information, %2Dend%20or%20open%2Dend.

CoreLogic (2012). *House price index May 2012.* https://www.corelogic.com/insights/home-price-index.aspx

Correspondents of *The New York Times.* (2005). *Class matters.* Times Books.

Cowan, S. P. (2006). Anti-snob land use laws, suburban exclusion, and housing opportunity. *Journal of Urban Affairs, 28*(3), 295–313.

Cromie, W., Kwasi, M., & Mihalik, A. (2017). Use of systemic risk exceptions for individual institutions during the financial crisis. In F. Carns (Ed.), *Crisis and response: An FDIC history, 2008–2013* (pp. 67–98). Federal Deposit Insurance Corporation.

Crossney, K. B., & Bartelt, D. W. (2005). The legacy of the Home Owners' Loan Corporation. *Housing Policy Debate, 16*(3–4), 547–574.

Crump, S., & Schuetz, J. (2021). *What the Great Recession can teach us about the post-pandemic housing market.* https://www.brookings.edu/articles/what-the-great-recession-can-teach-us-about-the-post-pandemic-housing-market/

Davidovich, Y., Reynolds, C. H., Kang, N., & Thomas, K. T. (2021). *Millennials and housing: Homeownership demographic research.* https://sf.freddiemac.com/docs/pdf/fact-sheet/millennial-playbook_millennials-and-housing.pdf

Day, J. C. (1996). *Projections of the number of households and families in the United States: 1995 to 2010.* https://www.census.gov/prod/1/pop/p25-1129.pdf

Dayen, D. (2016). *Chain of title: How three ordinary Americans uncovered Wall Street's great foreclosure fraud.* The New Press.

de la Campa, E. A., & Reina, V. J. (2023). Landlords' rental business before and after the COVID-19 pandemic: Evidence from a national cross-site survey. *Journal of Housing Economics, 59,* 101904.

Deng, L. (2007). Comparing the effects of Housing Vouchers and Low-Income Housing Tax Credits on neighborhood integration and school quality. *Journal of Planning Education and Research 27,* 20–35.

DePillis, L. (2022, September 27). Inflation has hit tenants hard. What about their landlords? https://www.nytimes.com/2022/09/27/business/economy/landlords-rent-inflation.html

Desmond, M. (2016). *Evicted: Poverty and profit in the American city.* Crown Publishing.

Desmond, M. (2023). *Poverty, by America.* Crown Publishing.

Detter, D. & Fölster, S. (2017). *The public wealth of cities: How to unlock hidden assets to boost growth and prosperity.* Brookings Institution Press.

Dettling, L. J., Hsu, J. W., Jacobs, L., Moore, K. B., & Thompson, J. P. (2017). *Recent trends in wealth-holding by race and ethnicity: Evidence from the Survey of Consumer Finances.* https://www.federalreserve.gov/econres/notes/feds-notes/recent-trends-in-wealth-holding-by-race-and-ethnicity-evidence-from-the-survey-of-consumer-finances-20170927.htm

Dexter, S. (1889). Co-operative savings and loan associations. *The Quarterly Journal of Economics, 3,* 315–335.

Dietrich, J., Liu, F., Skhirtladze, A., Davies, M., Jo, Y., & Candilis, C. (2019). *Data point: 2018 mortgage market activity and trends.* https://files.consumerfinance.gov/f/documents/cfpb_2018-mortgage-market-activity-trends_report.pdf

Dietz, R., & Haurin, D. (2003). The social and private micro-level consequences of homeownership. *Journal of Urban Economics, 54*(3), 401–450.

Dischinger, J. D. (2009). *Housing issues facing Somali refugees in Minneapolis, MN.* [Unpublished master's thesis]. University of Minnesota, Minneapolis, MN.

Doan, M. C. (1997). *American housing production: 1880–2000: A concise history.* University Press of America.

Dougherty, C. (2021). *Golden gates: The housing crisis and a reckoning for the American Dream.* Penguin.

Douglas, G. C. C. (2018). *The help-yourself city: Legitimacy and inequality in DIY urbanism.* Oxford University Press.

Dreier, P., Mollenkopf, J., & Swanstrom, T. (2014). *Place matters: Metropolitics for the twenty-first century.* University of Kansas Press.

Dynan, K., & Gayer, T. (2011). Government's role in the housing finance system: Where do we go from here? In M. N. Baily (Ed.), *The future of housing finance: Restructuring the U.S. residential mortgage market* (pp. 66–91). Brookings Institution Press.

Econometrica, Blake, K. S., Kellerson, R. L., & Simic, A. (2007). *Measuring overcrowding in housing.* https://www.huduser.gov/publications/pdf/measuring_overcrowding_in_hsg.pdf

Edelman, P. (2013). *So rich, so poor: Why it's so hard to end poverty in America.* The New Press.

Edin, K. J., & Shaefer, H. L. (2016). *$2 a day: Living on almost nothing in America.* Houghton Mifflin Harcourt.

Egan, M., Morrow, A., & Goldman, D. (2023, March 17). First Republic secures $30 billion rescue from large banks. https://edition.cnn.com/2023/03/16/investing/first-republic-bank/index.html

Emrath, P. (2020, April 1). National impact of home building and remodeling: Updated estimates. https://www.nahbclassic.org/fileUpload_details.aspx?contentTypeID=3&contentID=272642&subContentID=738975&channelID=311

Engel, K. C., & McCoy, P. A. (2011). *The subprime virus: Reckless credit, regulatory failure, and next steps.* Oxford University Press.

Enterprise Community Partners (n.d.). *What we do.* https://www.enterprisecommunity.org/about/what-we-do

Erickson, D. J. (2009). *The housing policy revolution: Networks and neighborhoods.* The Urban Institute Press.

Eviction Lab (n.d.). COVID-19 and changing eviction policies around the nation. https://evictionlab.org/covid-eviction-policies/

Fair Isaac Corporation (n.d.a). *What is a credit score?* https://www.myfico.com/credit-education/credit-scores

Fair Isaac Corporation (n.d.b). *What's in my FICO® scores?* https://www.myfico.com/credit-education/whats-in-your-credit-score

Fair Isaac Corporation (n.d.c). *How to repair your credit and improve your FICO® Scores.* https://www.myfico.com/credit-education/improve-your-credit-score

Fair Isaac Corporation (2019, July). *FICO® Score XD: Giving lenders the ability to identify creditworthy, previously unscorable borrowers.* https://www.fico.com/en/products/fico-score-xd

Fair Isaac Corporation (2021a, August 24). *More than 232 million US consumers can be scored by the FICO® score suite.* https://www.fico.com/blogs/more-232-million-us-consumers-can-be-scored-fico-score-suite

Fair Isaac Corporation (2021b). *Expanding credit access with alternative data: When used responsibly, untapped data sources can help score millions more consumers.* https://www.fico.com/en/resource-access/download/15431

Fallows, J., & Fallows, D. (2019). *Our towns: A 100,000-mile journey into the heart of America*. Vintage Books.

Fannie Mae (2023). *Equitable housing finance plan 2023*. https://www.fanniemae.com/about-us/esg/social/equitable-housing-finance-plan

Farley, R., Schuman, H., Bianchi, S., Colasanto, D., & Hatchett, S. (1978). "Chocolate City, Vanilla Suburbs": Will the trend toward racially separate communities continue? *Social Science Research*, 7(4), 319–344.

Federal Deposit Insurance Corporation (n.d.a). *Failed bank list*. https://www.fdic.gov/resources/resolutions/bank-failures/failed-bank-list/banklist.html

Federal Deposit Insurance Corporation (n.d.b). *Bank failures in brief*. https://www.fdic.gov/bank/historical/bank/

Federal Deposit Insurance Corporation (n.d.c). *Bank failures in brief – 2023*. https://www.fdic.gov/bank/historical/bank/bfb2023.html

Federal Financial Institutions Examination Council (2019). *A guide to HMDA reporting: Getting it right!* https://www.ffiec.gov/hmda/guide.htm

Federal Housing Administration (1939). *The structure and growth of residential neighborhoods in American cities*. Federal Housing Administration.

Federal Housing Finance Agency (n.d.a). *About FHFA: FHFA at-a-Glance*. https://www.fhfa.gov/AboutUs/Documents/FHFA%20At-A-Glance.pdf

Federal Housing Finance Agency (n.d.b). *Fannie Mae and Freddie Mac affordable housing goals*. https://www.fhfa.gov/PolicyProgramsResearch/Programs/AffordableHousing/Pages/Affordable-Housing-FNMandFRE.aspx

Federal Housing Finance Agency (n.d.c). *Housing goals performance*. https://www.fhfa.gov/PolicyProgramsResearch/Programs/AffordableHousing/Pages/Fannie-Mae-and-Freddie-Mac-Housing-Goals-Performance.aspx

Federal Register (2015, April 3). *Federal Housing Administration (FHA): Removal of Section 235 Home Ownership Program regulations*. https://www.federalregister.gov/documents/2015/04/03/2015-07597/federal-housing-administration-fha-removal-of-section-235-home-ownership-program-regulations

Federal Register (2019, September 12). *Notice of Neighborhood Stabilization Program: Changes to closeout requirements related to program income amendment*. https://www.federalregister.gov/documents/2019/09/12/2019-19708/notice-of-neighborhood-stabilization-program-changes-to-closeout-requirements-related-to-program

Federal Reserve Economic Data (n.d.a). *Median sales price of houses sold for the United States*. https://fred.stlouisfed.org/series/MSPUS

Federal Reserve Economic Data (n.d.b). *Real median household income in the United States*. https://fred.stlouisfed.org/series/MEHOINUSA672N

Federal Trade Commission (n.d.). Your equal credit opportunity rights. https://www.ftc.gov/enforcement/statutes/equal-credit-opportunity-act

Fischel, W. A. (2001). *The homevoter hypothesis: How home values influence local government taxation, school finance, and land-use policies*. Harvard University Press.

Fischel, W. A. (2015). *Zoning rules! The economics of land use regulation*. Lincoln Institute of Land Policy.

Fishback, P., Rose, J., & Snowden, K. (2013). *Well worth saving: How the New Deal safeguarded home ownership*. The University of Chicago Press.

Fisher, B., & Leite, F. (2018). *The cost of New York City's Hudson Yards redevelopment project*. https://www.economicpolicyresearch.org/images/docs/research/political_economy/Cost_of_Hudson_Yards_WP_11.5.18.pdf

Flanders, J. (2014). *The making of home: The 500-year story of how our houses became our homes*. St. Martin's Press.

Fogelson, R. M. (2001). *Downtown: Its rise and fall, 1880–1950*. Yale University Press.

Freddie Mac (n.d.). *30-year fixed-rate mortgages since 1971*. http://www.freddie-mac.com/pmms/pmms30.html

Freddie Mac (2022). *Equitable housing finance plan: Our commitment to making home possible equitably*. https://www.fhfa.gov/PolicyProgramsResearch/Programs/Documents/Freddie-2022-2024-EHFP.pdf

Freeman, L. (2019). *A haven and a hell: The ghetto in Black America*. Columbia University Press.

Freund, D. M. P. (2007). *Colored property: State policy and white racial politics in suburban America*. The University of Chicago Press.

Frey, W. H. (2018a). *Diversity explosion: How new racial demographics are remaking America*. Brookings Institution Press.

Frey, W. H. (2018b). *The millennial generation: A demographic bridge to America's diverse future*. https://www.brookings.edu/wp-content/uploads/2018/01/2018-jan_brookings-metro_millennials-a-demographic-bridge-to-americas-diverse-future.pdf

Frey, W. H. (2018c). *The US will become "minority white" in 2045, Census projects: Youthful minorities are the engine of future growth*. https://www.brookings.edu/blog/the-avenue/2018/03/14/the-us-will-become-minority-white-in-2045-census-projects/

Frey, W. H. (2018d). *21st century immigration favors Asians and college grads as the US foreign-born share rises*. https://www.brookings.edu/blog/the-avenue/2018/09/24/21st-century-immigration-favors-asians-and-college-grads-as-the-us-foreign-born-share-rises/

Fry, R. (2020, April 28). *Millennials overtake baby boomers as America's largest generation*. https://www.pewresearch.org/short-reads/2020/04/28/millennials-overtake-baby-boomers-as-americas-largest-generation/

Galante, C. (2013a). *Written testimony of Assistant Secretary for Housing and Federal Housing Administration Carol Galante: Hearing before the House Financial Services Committee*. https://archives.hud.gov/testimony/2013/060413senateappropswf.pdf

Galante, C. (2013b, September 27). *Letter to The Honorable Tim Johnson and The Honorable Mike Crapo*. http://online.wsj.com/public/resources/documents/FHA.pdf

Galante, C. (2017). *Mission critical: Retooling FHA to meet America's housing needs.* http://ternercenter.berkeley.edu/uploads/FHA_Reform_Proposal_Paper_FINAL_REVISED_01-22-2018.pdf

Galster, G. C. (2019). *Making our neighborhoods, making our selves.* The University of Chicago Press.

Garriga, C., Ricketts, L. R., & Schlagenhauf, D. E. (2017). The homeownership experience of minorities during the Great Recession. *Federal Reserve Bank of St. Louis Review, 99*(1), 139–167.

Geisst, C. R. (2017). *Loan sharks: The birth of predatory lending.* Brookings Institution Press.

Geithner, T. F. (2014). *Stress test: Reflections on financial crises.* Crown.

Gissler, S., & Narajabad, B. (2017a). *The increased role of the Federal Home Loan Bank System in funding markets: Part 1: Background.* https://www.federalreserve.gov/econres/notes/feds-notes/the-increased-role-of-the-federal-home-loan-bank-system-in-funding-markets-part-1-background-20171018.htm

Gissler, S., & Narajabad, B. (2017b). *The increased role of the Federal Home Loan Bank System in funding markets: Part 2: Recent trends and potential drivers.* https://www.federalreserve.gov/econres/notes/feds-notes/the-increased-role-of-the-federal-home-loan-bank-system-in-funding-markets-part-2-20171018.html

Gissler, S., & Narajabad, B. (2017c). *The increased role of the Federal Home Loan Bank System in funding markets: Part 3: Implications for financial stability.* https://www.federalreserve.gov/econres/notes/feds-notes/the-increased-role-of-the-federal-home-loan-bank-system-in-funding-markets-part-3-20171018.htm

Glaeser, E., & Gyourko, J. (2018). The economic implications of housing supply. *Journal of Economic Perspectives, 32*(1), 3–30.

Glantz, A. (2019) *Homewreckers: How a gang of Wall Street kingpins, hedge fund magnates, crooked banks, and vulture capitalists suckered millions out of their homes and demolished the American Dream.* Custom House.

Goetz, E. (2012). HOPE VI. In A. T. Carswell (Ed.), *The encyclopedia of housing* (pp. 303–306). SAGE.

Goetz, E. (2013). *New Deal ruins: Race, economic justice, and public housing policy.* Cornell University Press.

Golding, E., Goodman, L., Walsh, J., & Choi, J. H. (2021, February). *The preferred stock purchase agreements will hamper access to credit.* https://www.urban.org/research/publication/preferred-stock-purchase-agreements-will-hamper-access-credit

Golding, E. L., Szymanoski, E. J., & Lee, P. P. (2014). *FHA at 80: Preparing for the future.* https://www.huduser.gov/portal/publications/fha/fhaat80.html

Goodman, L. S. (2017). Quantifying the tightness of mortgage credit and assessing policy actions. https://www.urban.org/research/publication/quantifying-tightness-mortgage-credit-and-assessing-policy-actions

Goodman, L. S., & Mayer, C. (2018). Homeownership and the American Dream. *Journal of Economic Perspectives, 32*(1), 31–58.

Goodman, L., McCargo, A., Golding, E., Parrott, J., Pardo, S., Hill-Jones, T. M., Kaul, K., Strochak, S., Reyes, A., & Walsh, J. (2019a, July). *Housing finance at a glance: A monthly chartbook.* Urban Institute.

Goodman, L., McCargo, A., Golding, E., Parrott, J., Pardo, S., Hill-Jones, T. M., Kaul, K., Strochak, S., Walsh, J., Rincon, A., & Young, C. (2019b, August). *Housing finance at a glance: A monthly chartbook.* Urban Institute.

Goodman, L., McCargo, A., Parrott, J., Zhu, J. Pardo, S., Kaul, K., Neal, M., Choi, J., Strochak, S., Walsh, J., Young, C., & Rincon, A. (2020, February). *Housing finance at a glance: A monthly chartbook.* https://www.urban.org/research/publication/housing-finance-glance-monthly-chartbook-february-2020

Goodman, L., McCargo, A., Seidman, E., Parrott, J., Pardo, S., Hill, T., Zhu, J. Bai, B., Kaul, K., Woluchem, M., Ganesh, B., & Rincon, A. (2017, May). *Housing finance at a glance: A monthly chartbook.* https://edit.urban.org/sites/default/files/publication/90451/may_chartbook.pdf

Goodman, L., & Neal, M. (2022). How higher mortgage rates have historically affected home prices. https://www.urban.org/urban-wire/how-higher-mortgage-rates-have-historically-affected-home-prices

Goodman, L., Zhu, J., & George, T. (2015). *The impact of tight credit standards on 2009–2013 lending.* http://www.urban.org/sites/default/files/publication/48731/2000165-The-Impact-of-Tight-Credit-Standards-on-2009-13-Lending.pdf

Goodman, L., Zhu, L., Visalli, K., Seidman, E., & Zhu, J. (2023). An assessment of lending to LMI and minority neighborhoods and borrowers. https://www.urban.org/research/publication/assessment-lending-lmi-and-minority-neighborhoods-and-borrowers

Gramlich, E. (2022). *Housing choice vouchers.* https://nlihc.org/sites/default/files/2022-03/2022AG_4-01_Housing-Choice-Vouchers.pdf

Granovetter, M. (1973). The strength of weak ties. *American Journal of Sociology, 78*(6), 1360–1380.

Graves, E., Muñoz, A. P., Hamilton, D., Darity, W. A., & Nam, Y. (2020). Non-Hispanic White versus Black parental wealth and wealth transfers to enable homeownership in five metropolitan areas. In K. B. Anacker, M. T. Nguyen, & D. P. Varady (Eds.), *The Routledge handbook of housing policy and planning* (pp. 54–67). Routledge.

Greenlee, A. J. (2020). Redefining rental housing choice in the Housing Choice Voucher Program. In K. B. Anacker, M. T. Nguyen, & D. P. Varady (Eds.), *The Routledge handbook of housing policy and planning* (pp. 141–154). Routledge.

Griffith, J. (2012). *The Federal Housing Administration saved the housing market.* https://www.americanprogress.org/issues/economy/reports/2012/10/11/40824/the-federal-housing-administration-saved-the-housing-market/

Gruenberg, M. J. (2023, March 28). *Statement of Martin J. Gruenberg, Chairman, Federal Deposit Insurance Corporation, on recent bank failures and the federal regulatory response before the Committee on Banking, Housing, and Urban Affairs, United States Senate.* https://www.fdic.gov/news/speeches/2023/spmar2923.html

Gura, D. (2023, March 16). *First Republic becomes the latest bank to be rescued, this time by its rivals.* https://www.npr.org/2023/03/16/1163958533/first-republic-bank-silicon-valley-bank-signature-bank-bank-run

Hadjiyanni, T. (2007). Bounded choices: Somali women constructing difference in Minnesota housing. *Journal of Interior Design, 32*(2), 13–27.

Hagerty, J. (2012). *The fateful history of Fannie Mae: New Deal birth to mortgage crisis fail.* The History Press.

Harrington, M. (2012). *The other America: Poverty in the United States.* Scribner.

Harris, A. (2016). *A pound of flesh: Monetary sanctions as punishment for the poor.* Russell Sage Foundation.

Harris, R. (1996) *Unplanned suburbs: Toronto's American tragedy 1900 to 1950.* The Johns Hopkins University Press.

Harris, R. (2012). *Building a market: The rise of the home improvement industry, 1914–1960.* The University of Chicago Press.

Harrison, A., & Immergluck, D. (2021). Housing vacancy and hypervacant neighborhoods: Uneven recovery after the U.S. foreclosure crisis. *Journal of Urban Affairs, 45*(8), 1469–1485.

Hartje, S. C., Ewen, H. H., & Tremblay, K. R. (2018). Universal design in housing. In K. B. Anacker, A. T. Carswell, S. D. Kirby, & K. R. Tremblay (Eds.), *Introduction to housing* (pp. 98–117). University of Georgia Press.

Hartman, C. (1992). Debating the Low-Income Housing Tax Credit: Feeding the sparrows by feeding the horses. *Shelterforce*, January/February, n.p.

Hashimzade, N., Myles, G., & Black. J. (2017). *A dictionary of economics.* Oxford University Press.

Hayes, A. (2020, March 10). *Austerity.* https://www.investopedia.com/terms/a/austerity.asp

Hays, R. A. (2012). *The Federal Government and urban housing.* State University of New York Press.

HealthCare.gov (n.d.). *How insurance companies set health premiums.* https://www.healthcare.gov/how-plans-set-your-premiums/

Heathcott, J. (2015). Myth #1: Public housing stands alone. In N. D. Bloom, F. Umbach, & L. J. Vale (Eds.), *Public housing myths: Perception, reality, and social policy* (pp. 31–46). Cornell University Press.

Hepburn, P., Louis, R., Fish, J., Lemmerman, E., Alexander, A. K., Thomas, T. A., Koehler, R., Benfer, E., & Desmond, M. (2021). U.S. eviction filing patterns in 2020. *Socius, 7*, 1–18.

Hetzel, R. L. (2012). *The Great Recession: Market failure or policy failure?* Cambridge University Press.

Highsmith, A. R. (2015). *Demolition means progress: Flint, Michigan, and the fate of the American metropolis.* The University of Chicago Press.

Housing Act of 1949 (Section 2 and Title V).

Housing Finance Policy Center (2019, July 16). *Housing Credit Availability Index.* https://www.urban.org/policy-centers/housing-finance-policy-center/projects/housing-credit-availability-index

Housing Trust Fund Project (n.d.). What are housing trust funds? https://housingtrustfundproject.org/

Howard, E. (2013). *Homeless: Poverty and place in urban America.* University of Pennsylvania Press.

Howard, T. (2014). *The mortgage wars: Inside Fannie Mae, big-money politics, and the collapse of the American Dream.* McGraw-Hill.

Howell, K. (2018). Housing and community. In K. B. Anacker, A. T. Carswell, S. D. Kirby, & K. R. Tremblay (Eds.), *Introduction to housing* (pp. 199–217). University of Georgia Press.

Hunt, D. B. (2015). Myth #2: Modernist architecture failed public housing. In N. D. Bloom, F. Umbach, & L. J. Vale (Eds.), *Public housing myths: Perception, reality, and social policy* (pp. 47–63). Cornell University Press.

Huynh, F. (2012, September 2011). Do credit scores have a disparate impact on racial minorities? https://www.fico.com/blogs/do-credit-scores-have-disparate-impact-racial-minorities

Iglesias, T. (2009). Our pluralist ethics and public-private partnerships for affordable housing. In N. M. Davidson & R. P. Malloy (Eds.), *Affordable housing and public-private partnerships* (pp. 11–33). Routledge.

Immergluck, D. (2011). From minor to major player: The geography of FHA lending during the U.S. mortgage crisis. *Journal of Urban Affairs, 33*(1), 1–20.

Immergluck, D. (2013). Too little, too late, and too timid: The federal response to the foreclosure crisis at the five-year mark. *Housing Policy Debate, 23*(1), 199–232.

Institute for Women's Policy Research (2017). *Status of women in the states: Projected year the wage gap will close by state.* http://statusofwomendata.org/wp-content/uploads/2017/06/R476.pdf

Internal Revenue Service (n.d.). *Publication 936 (2018): Home mortgage interest deduction.* https://www.irs.gov/forms-pubs/about-publication-936

International Monetary Fund (2020, April). *World economic outlook.* https://www.imf.org/en/Publications/WEO/Issues/2020/04/14/weo-april-2020

Jackson, K. T. (1985). *Crabgrass frontier: The suburbanization of the United States.* Oxford University Press.

Jacobs, J. (1961). *The death and life of great American cities.* Vintage Books.

Jacobus, R. (2015). *Inclusionary housing: Creating and maintaining equitable communities.* Lincoln Institute of Land Policy.

Johnson, D. A. (1996). *Planning the great metropolis: The 1929 Regional Plan of New York and its environs.* Routledge.

Johnson, J. A. (1996). *Showing America a new way home: Expanding opportunities for home ownership.* Jossey-Bass Publishers.

Johnson, S., & Kwak, J. (2010). *Thirteen bankers: The Wall Street takeover and the next financial meltdown.* Pantheon Books.

Joint Center for Housing Studies of Harvard University (2023). *The state of the nation's housing 2023.* https://www.jchs.harvard.edu/state-nations-housing-2023

Jones, K. (2019). *FHA-insured home loans: An overview.* https://fas.org/sgp/crs/misc/RS20530.pdf

Katz, A. (2009). *Our lot: How real estate came to own us.* Bloomsbury.

Katz, B., & Nowak, J. (2017). *The new localism: How cities can thrive in the age of populism.* Brookings Institution Press.

Katz, L., & Zhao, C. (2023, February 22). U.S. homeowners have lost $2.3 trillion in value since June peak. https://www.redfin.com/news/housing-market-loses-value-2023/

Katznelson, I. (2005). *When affirmative action was White: An untold history of racial inequality in twentieth-century America.* W. W. Norton.

Kawitzky, S., Freiberg, F., Houk, D. L., & Hankins, S. (2013). *Choice constrained, segregation maintained: Using federal tax credits to provide affordable housing.* https://www.fairhousingjustice.org/wp-content/uploads/2013/08/FHJC-LIHTCREPORT-Aug13-Fullv1-7-WEB.pdf

Kaysen, R. (2023, July 9). The modern farmhouse is today's McMansion: And it's here to stay. *The New York Times.*

Keating, W. D. (1998). Rent regulation in New York City: A protracted saga. In W. D. Keating, M. Teitz, & A. Skaburskis (Eds.), *Rent control: Regulation and the rental housing market* (pp. 151–168). Center for Urban Policy Research.

Keating, W. D. (2012). Community development corporations. In A. T. Carswell (Ed.), *The encyclopedia of housing* (pp. 68–70). SAGE.

Keating, W. D. (2020). The right to housing: The goal versus the reality. In K. B. Anacker, M. T. Nguyen, & D. P. Varady (Eds.), *The Routledge handbook of housing policy and planning* (pp. 11–22). Routledge.

Keefer, A. (2018, December 19). Where does the money from property taxes go? *SFGate.*

Keightley, M. P. (2020). *An economic analysis of the Mortgage Interest Deduction.* https://crsreports.congress.gov/product/details?prodcode=R46429

Kinder, K. (2016). *DIY Detroit: Making do in a city without services.* University of Minnesota Press.

Kirby, S. D., & Hardison-Moody, A. (2018). Housing and disasters. In K. B. Anacker, A. T. Carswell, S. D. Kirby, & K. R. Tremblay (Eds.), *Introduction to housing* (pp. 356–374). University of Georgia Press.

Kirsch, L., & Squires, G. D. (2017). *Meltdown: The financial crisis, consumer protection, and the road forward.* Praeger.

Kislev, E. (2019). *Happy singlehood: The rising acceptance and celebration of solo living.* University of California Press.

Klinenberg, E. (2012). *Going solo: The extraordinary rise and surprising appeal of living alone.* Penguin.

Kneebone, E., & Berube, A. (2013). *Confronting suburban poverty in America.* Brookings Institution Press.

Koch, J. V. (2019). *The impoverishment of the American college student.* Brookings Institution Press.

Kotlowitz, A. (1991). *There are no children here: The story of two boys growing up in the other America.* Anchorbooks/Doubleday.

Kramer, A., Eisen, J., Garden, N., Gunning, J., Gunter, G. R., Hutensky, B. M., Jones, J., Long, C. A., McCauley, M., Moore, M. A., Nasuti, S., Peloquin, R., Tschiderer, J. R., Whitney, W. H., Wright, M., Dale, R., Enlow, C., Fader, S., Fox, M. K., … Takesuye, D. (2008). *Retail development.* Urban Land Institute.

Kusenbach, M., & Paulsen, K. E. (Eds.). (2013). *Home: International perspectives on culture, identity, and belonging.* Peter Lang.

Landis, J. (2012). President's Committee on Urban Housing (Kaiser Commission). In A. T. Carswell (Ed.), *The encyclopedia of housing* (pp. 557–559). SAGE.

Lane, B. (2019, October 3). Fannie Mae and Freddie Mac now appear to be here to stay. How exactly did that happen? Not too long ago, Congress was trying to shut the GSEs down. *Housing Wire.*

Lang, H., & Chakroborti, A. (2023, March 8). Crypto-focused bank Silvergate plans to wind down following blow from FTX. https://www.reuters.com/technology/crypto-focused-bank-silvergate-plans-wind-down-operations-2023-03-08/

Law, J. (2018). *A dictionary of finance and banking.* Oxford University Press.

Layton, D. (2021). *The homeownership rate and housing finance policy: Part 1: Learning from the rate's history.* https://www.jchs.harvard.edu/research-areas/working-papers/homeownership-rate-and-housing-finance-policy-part-1-learning-rates

Leonard, C. (2022). *The lords of easy money: How the Federal Reserve broke the American economy.* Simon & Schuster.

Levenstein, L. (2015). Myth #11: Tenants did not invest in public housing. In N. D. Bloom, F. Umbach, & L. J. Vale (Eds.), *Public housing myths: Perception, reality, and social policy* (pp. 223–234). Cornell University Press.

Levy, J. M. (2006). *Contemporary urban planning.* Pearson Prentice Hall.

Lewis, H. (2023, June 14). *How the Federal Reserve affects mortgage rates: The Federal Reserve is one of many influences on mortgage rates, along with inflation and economic growth.* https://www.nerdwallet.com/article/mortgages/fed-mortgage-rates

Lopez, M. H., & Passel, J. (2015). *Modern immigration wave brings 59 million to U.S., driving population growth and change through 2065: Views of immigration's impact on U.S. society mixed.* https://www.pewresearch.org/hispanic/2015/09/28/modern-immigration-wave-brings-59-million-to-u-s-driving-population-growth-and-change-through-2065/

Lopez, R. (2012). *Building American public health: Urban planning, architecture, and the quest for better health in the United States.* Palgrave Macmillan.

Lowi, T. J. (1972). Four systems of policy, politics, and choice. *Public Administration Review, 32*(4), 298–310.

Lung-Amam, W. S. (2020). A new generation of "single-family" homes: Multigenerational homebuilding in the suburbs of Phoenix, Arizona. In K. B. Anacker, M. T. Nguyen, & D. P. Varady (Eds.), *The Routledge handbook of housing policy and planning* (pp. 357–371). Routledge.

Mallach, A. (2012). Mount Laurel. In A. T. Carswell (Ed.), *The encyclopedia of housing* (pp. 483–486). SAGE.

Mallach, A. (2018). *The empty house next door: Understanding and reducing vacancy and hypervacancy in the United States.* Lincoln Institute of Land Policy.

Manturuk, K. R., Lindblad, M. R., & Quercia, R. G. (2017). *A place called home: The social dimensions of homeownership.* Oxford University Press.

Marvell, T. B. (1969). *The Federal Home Loan Bank board.* Frederick A. Praeger, Publishers.

Maslow, A. (1970). *Motivation and personality.* Harper & Row.

Mason, D. L. (2004). *From Buildings and Loans to bail-outs: A history of the American savings and loan industry.* Cambridge University Press.

Massey, D., Albright, L., Casciano, R., Derickson, E., & Kinsey, D. N. (2013). *Climbing Mount Laurel: The struggle for affordable housing and social mobility in an American suburb.* Princeton University Press.

McCabe, B. J. (2016). *No place like home: Wealth, community, and the politics of homeownership.* Oxford University Press.

McClure, K. (2018). Federal housing policy. In K. B. Anacker, A. T. Carswell, S. D. Kirby, & K. R. Tremblay (Eds.), *Introduction to housing* (pp. 235–254). University of Georgia Press.

McClure, K. (2020). Subsidized rental housing programs in the U.S.: A case of rising expectations. In K. B. Anacker, M. T. Nguyen, & D. P. Varady (Eds.), *The Routledge handbook of housing policy and planning* (pp. 129–140). Routledge.

McClure, K., & Schwartz, A. (2023, June 30). Homes are expensive: Building more won't solve the problem. https://www.barrons.com/articles/housing-crisis-build-more-homes-1342c24f?refsec=real-estate&mod=topics_real-estate&fbclid=IwAR0ZPpvPA8RTBVFePiFqkDKctpOY-DonGsy9CNB809xXv-m7-w1ZzdXBXt_w

McGhee, F. (2018, September 5). The most important housing law passed in 1968 wasn't the Fair Housing Act. https://shelterforce.org/2018/09/05/the-most-important-housing-law-passed-in-1968-wasnt-the-fair-housing-act/

Mendenhall, E. (2018). Retail follows rooftops: Commercial real estate and the importance of fair housing: A note from the President, Elizabeth Mendenhall. https://www.nar.realtor/commercial-connections/retail-follows-rooftops-commercial-real-estate-the-importance-of-fair-housing-a-note-from-the

Meschede, T., Morgan, J., Aurand, A., & Threet, D. (2021). *Misdirected housing supports: Why the Mortgage Interest Deduction unjustly subsidizes high-income households and expands racial disparities.* https://nlihc.org/sites/default/files/NLIHC-IERE_MID-Report.pdf

Metzger, J. T. (1998). Home Owners' Loan Corporation. In W. van Vliet (Ed.), *The encyclopedia of housing* (pp. 232–233). SAGE.

Millstone, E., & Lang, T. (2013). *The atlas of food: Who eats what, where, and why.* University of California Press.

Mishel, L., Bivens, J., Gould, E., & Shierholz, H. (2012). *The state of working America.* ILR Press.

Mogilnicki, E. J., & Malpass, M. S. (2013). The first year of the Consumer Financial Protection Bureau: An overview. *The Business Lawyer, 68*(2), 557–570.

Moore, N. Y. (2016). *The South Side: A portrait of Chicago and American segregation.* Picador.

Moos, M., Pfeiffer, D., & Vinodrai, T. (Eds.). (2018). *The millennial city: Trends, implications, and prospects for urban planning and policy.* Routledge.

Morduch, J., & Schneider, R. (2017). *The financial diaries: How American families cope in a world of uncertainty.* Princeton University Press.

Mudde, C., & Kaltwasser, C. R. (2017). *Populism: A very short introduction.* Oxford University Press.

Muro, M., Liu, S., Whiton, J., & Kulkarni, S. (2017). *Digitalization and the American workforce.* https://www.brookings.edu/research/digitalization-and-the-american-workforce/

Murphy, S. L., Xu, J. Q., Kochanek, K. D., & Arias, E. (2018, November). *Mortality in the United States, 2017.* https://www.cdc.gov/nchs/products/databriefs/db328.htm

Myerson, D. L. (2016). *How did they do it? Discovering new opportunities for affordable housing.* National Association of Home Builders.

National Alliance to End Homelessness (2016). *Fact sheet: Housing First.* http://endhomelessness.org/wp-content/uploads/2016/04/housing-first-fact-sheet.pdf

National Association of Home Builders (n.d.). *NAHB/Wells Fargo Housing Market Index (HMI).* https://www.nahb.org/News-and-Economics/Housing-Economics/Indices/Housing-Market-Index#:~:text=The%20NAHB%2F-Wells%20Fargo%20Housing, the%20single%2Dfamily%20housing%20market.

National Association of Home Builders (2015a). *The economic impact of home building in a typical state: Income, jobs, and taxes generated.* https://www.nahb.org/-/media/NAHB/news-and-economics/docs/housing-economics/economic-impact/economic-impact-local-area-2015.pdf

National Association of Home Builders (2015b). *The economic impact of home building in a typical state: Comparing costs to revenue for state and local governments.* https://www.nahb.org/-/media/NAHB/news-and-economics/docs/housing-economics/economic-impact/economic-impact-local-area-comparing-costs-2015.pdf

National Bureau of Economic Research (n.d.). *U.S. business cycle expansions and contractions.* https://www.nber.org/cycles.html

National Center for Health Statistics (2022). *Mortality in the United States, 2021.* https://www.cdc.gov/nchs

National Commission on the Causes of the Financial and Economic Crisis in the United States (2011). *The financial crisis inquiry report.* Public Affairs.

National Council of State Housing Agencies (n.d.). HOME Investment Partnerships Program 2023 FAQs. https://www.ncsha.org/wp-content/uploads/2018/01/HOME-Investment-Partnerships-Program-FAQs-2023.pdf

National Fire Protection Association (n.d.). *Public education: Top fire causes.* https://www.nfpa.org/Public-Education/Fire-causes-and-risks#:~:-text=Top%20fire%20causes%20Cooking%2C%20heating, electrical%2C%20smoking%2C%20and%20candles.

National Low Income Housing Coalition (2019, October 17). *Public housing: Where do we stand?* https://nlihc.org/resource/public-housing-where-do-we-stand

Nelson, A. C. (2013). *Reshaping metropolitan America: Development trends and opportunities to 2030.* Island Press.

Newman, K. S. (2012). *The accordion family: Boomerang kids, anxious parents, and the private toll of global competition.* Beacon Press.

New York State (n.d.). *Homes and community renewal: NYS HOME local program.* https://hcr.ny.gov/nys-home-program

NYU Furman Center (2018a). *NYCHA's outsized role in housing New York's poorest households.* https://furmancenter.org/news/press-release/report-nychas-outsized-role-in-housing-new-yorks-poorest-households

NYU Furman Center (2018b). *State of New York City's subsidized housing in 2017.* https://furmancenter.org/thestoop/entry/the-state-of-new-york-citys-subsidized-housing

Ocejo, R. E. (2017). *Masters of craft: Old jobs in the new urban economy.* Princeton University Press.

Oldenburg, R. (1999). *The great good place: Cafes, coffee shops, bookstores, bars, hair salons, and other hangouts at the heart of a community.* Marlowe & Company.

Olshansky, S. J., Antonucci, T., Berkman, L., Binstock, R. H., Boersch-Supan, A., Cacioppo, J. T., Carnes, B. A., Carstensen, L. L., Fried, L. P., Goldman, D. P., Jackson, J., Kohli, M., Rother, J., Zheng, Y., & Rowe, J. (2012). Differences in life expectancy due to race and educational differences are widening, and many may not catch up. *Health Affairs, 31*(8), 1803–1813.

Parker, K., & Barroso, A. (2021, February 25). *In Vice President Kamala Harris, we can see how America has changed.* https://www.pewresearch.org/short-reads/2021/02/25/in-vice-president-kamala-harris-we-can-see-how-america-has-changed/

Parker, K., & Patten, E. (2013, January 30). *The sandwich generation: Rising financial burdens for middle-aged Americans.* https://www.pewsocialtrends.org/2013/01/30/the-sandwich-generation/

Parrott, J., & Zandi, M. (2021). *Averting an eviction crisis.* https://www.moodysanalytics.com/-/media/article/2021/averting-an-eviction-crisis.pdf

Parrott, K. P., & Atiles, J. H. (2018). Home environments and health. In K. B. Anacker, A. T. Carswell, S. D. Kirby, & K. R. Tremblay (Eds.), *Introduction to housing* (pp. 316–340). University of Georgia Press.

Parrott, K. P., & Beamish, J. O. (2018). Kitchen and bathroom design. In K. B. Anacker, A. T. Carswell, S. D. Kirby, & K. R. Tremblay (Eds.), *Introduction to housing* (pp. 43–63). University of Georgia Press.

Pendall, R., Hendey, L., Greenberg, D., Pettit, K. L. S., Levy, D., Khare, A., Gallagher, M., Joseph, M., Curley, A., Rasheed, A., Latham, N., Brecher, A., & Hailey, C. (2015). *Choice Neighborhoods: Baseline conditions and early progress.* U.S. Department of Housing and Urban Development.

Pendleton, J. H., Marzullo, C., Kruse, B., Anderson, M., Brown, A., Chaidez, L., Devaney, G. Fisher, J., Gillich, T., McGrail, J., Molino, M., Schwab, E., Sowash, S., Rabe, M., & Stone, F. (2021, March). *COVID-19 housing protections: Moratoriums have helped limit evictions, but further outreach is needed.* https://www.gao.gov/products/gao-21-370

Peterson, S. J. (2013). *Planning the home front: Building bombers and communities at Willow Run.* The University of Chicago Press.

Pfeiffer, D., Anacker, K. B., & Louton, B. (2016). *What are the effects of doubling up on retirement income and assets?* https://crr.bc.edu/working-papers/what-are-the-effects-of-doubling-up-on-retirement-income-and-assets-2/

Philp, D. (2017). *A $500 house in Detroit: Rebuilding an abandoned home and an American city.* Simon & Schuster.

Pilkauskas, N. V. (2012). Three-generation family households: Differences by family structure at birth. *Journal of Marriage and Family, 74*(October), 931–943.

Piquet, H. S. (1930). *Building and loan associations in New Jersey.* Princeton University Press.

Plunz, R. (2016). *A history of housing in New York City.* Columbia University Press.

Popkin, S. J. (2018). The limits of housing revitalization as a platform for improving residents' economic well-being: Lessons from the U.S. *International Journal of Urban Sciences, 22*(4), 461–472.

Pozen, R. C. (2011). Toward a three-tier market for U.S. home mortgages. In M. N. Baily (Ed.), *The future of housing finance: Restructuring the U.S. residential mortgage market* (pp. 26–65). Brookings Institution Press.

Prevost, L. (2013). *Snob zones: Fear, prejudice, and real estate.* Beacon Press.

Proctor, E. M. (2012). Right to housing. In A. T. Carswell (Ed.), *Encyclopedia of housing* (pp. 639–642). SAGE.

Quart, A. (2018). *Squeezed: Why our families can't afford America*. Ecco.

Ramirez, K. (2019a, September 12). Trump administration working to end Fannie/Freddie profit sweep in September: Actively negotiating new Fannie, Freddie amendment. *Housing Wire*.

Ramirez, K. (2019b, September 30). Treasury to allow Fannie Mae, Freddie Mac to retain $45 million in capital: Administration takes next step in housing reform. *Housing Wire*.

Rascoff, S., & Humphries, S. (2015). *Zillow talk: The new rules of real estate*. Grand Central Publishing.

Ratcliffe, C., & Brown, S. (2017, November 20). *Credit scores perpetuate racial disparities, even in America's most prosperous cities*. https://www.urban.org/urban-wire/credit-scores-perpetuate-racial-disparities-even-americas-most-prosperous-cities

Ratcliffe, J., Stegman, M., & Reynolds, K. (2022, June). *The FHFA's Equitable Housing Finance Plans for Fannie Mae and Freddie Mac: Equity should be a primary business consideration for the GSEs*. https://www.urban.org/research/publication/fhfas-equitable-housing-finance-plans-fannie-mae-and-freddie-mac-equity-should-be-primary-business-consideration-gses

RealtyTrac (2013). *U.S. foreclosure inventory increases 9 percent from year ago in first quarter*. https://wpnewsroom.realtytrac.com/news/foreclosure-trends/page/13/

Reid, C. K. (2020). Homeownership and the racial and ethnic wealth gap in the United States. In K. B. Anacker, M. T. Nguyen, & D. P. Varady (Eds.), *The Routledge handbook of housing policy and planning* (pp. 37–53). Routledge.

Reinhart, C. M., & Rogoff, K. S. (2009). *This time is different: Eight centuries of financial folly*. Princeton University Press.

Reiss, D. (2011). *Fannie Mae, Freddie Mac, and the future of federal housing finance policy: A study of regulatory privilege*. https://www.cato.org/publications/policy-analysis/fannie-mae-freddie-mac-future-federal-housing-finance-policy-study-regulatory-privilege-0

Revell, K. D. (2003). *Building Gotham: Civic culture and policy in New York City, 1898–1938*. The Johns Hopkins University Press.

Riegel, R., & Doubman, J. R. (1927). *The building-and-loan association*. John Wiley & Sons.

Riismandel, K. (2020). *Neighborhood of fear: The suburban crisis in American culture, 1975–2001*. The Johns Hopkins University Press.

Riquier, A. (2017, January 21). *Trump already suspends Obama-era FHA mortgage insurance cut*. https://www.marketwatch.com/story/trump-already-suspends-obama-era-fha-mortgage-insurance-cut-2017-01-20

Roberts, A. (2012). *America's first great depression: Economic crisis and political disorder after the panic of 1837*. Cornell University Press.

Robinson, K. J. (2013). *Savings and loan crisis: 1980–1989: In the 1980s, the financial sector suffered through a period of distress that was focused on the nation's savings and loan industry*. https://www.federalreservehistory.org/essays/savings_and_loan_crisis

Rodriguez, J. (2023, May 10). *Why are rents still sky-high? Because people ditched their roommates*. https://www.businessinsider.com/why-apartment-rent-high-pandemic-big-cities-household-formation-roommates-2023-5

Rohe, W. (2012). Homeownership. In A. T. Carswell (Ed.), *The encyclopedia of housing* (pp. 293–298). SAGE.

Rosenbaum, D., Bergh, K., & Hall, L. (2023, February 6). Temporary pandemic SNAP benefits will end in remaining 35 states in March 2023. https://www.cbpp.org/research/food-assistance/temporary-pandemic-snap-benefits-will-end-in-remaining-35-states-in-march

Rothstein, R. (2017). *The color of law: A forgotten history of how our government segregated America*. W. W. Morton.

Rothstein, R. (2023). Could more bank failures trigger a housing market crash? https://www.forbes.com/advisor/mortgages/could-recent-bank-failures-trigger-housing-market-crash/#:~:text=Though%20housing%20market%20watchers%20acknowledge, housing%20market%20crash%20is%-20low.

Roubini, N., & Mihm, S. (2011). *Crisis economics: A crash course in the future of finance*. Penguin Books.

Rouse, C., Bernstein, J., Kundsen, H., & Zhang, Z. (2021, June 17). *Exclusionary zoning: Its effect on racial discrimination in the housing market*. https://www.whitehouse.gov/cea/written-materials/2021/06/17/exclusionary-zoning-its-effect-on-racial-discrimination-in-the-housing-market/

Ruggles, S. (2007). The decline of intergenerational coresidence in the United States, 1850 to 2000. *American Sociological Review, 72*(6), 964–989.

Rybczynski, W. (2007). *Last harvest: How a cornfield became New Daleville: Real estate development in America from George Washington to the builders of the twenty-first century, and why we live in houses anyway*. Scribner.

Salamon, S., & MacTavish, K. (2017). *Singlewide: Chasing the American Dream in a rural trailer park*. Cornell University Press.

Sanbonmatsu, L., Ludwig, J., Katz, L. F., Gennetian, L. A., Duncan, G. J., Kessler, R. C., Adam, E., McDade, T. W., & Lindau, S. T. (2011). Moving to Opportunity for Fair Housing Demonstration Program: Final impacts evaluation. https://www.huduser.gov/portal/publications/pubasst/MTOFHD.html

Santarelli, M. (2023, July 1). Bank failures 2023: Will collapse affect housing market? https://www.noradarealestate.com/blog/bank-failures/#:~:text=-The%20collapse%20of%20banks%20can, which%20fuels%20the%20housing%20market.

Sassler, S., & Miller, A. J. (2017). *Cohabitation nation: Gender, class, and the remaking of relationships*. University of California Press.

Satter, B. (2009). *Family properties: How the struggle over race and real estate transformed Chicago and urban America*. Picador.

Scharfstein, D., & Sunderam, A. (2011). The economics of housing finance reform. In M. N. Baily (Ed.), *The future of housing finance: Restructuring the U.S. residential mortgage market* (pp. 146–197). Brookings Institution Press.

Scally, C. P., Anoli, C. H., Choi, J., Spauster, P., Hendey, L., Levy, D. K., & Bai, B. (2018). *Responding to a crisis: The National Foreclosure Mitigation Counseling Program 2008–2018.* https://www.urban.org/research/publication/responding-crisis-national-foreclosure-mitigation-counseling-program-2008-2018

Scally, C. P., Gold, A., & DuBois, N. (2018). The Low-Income Housing Tax Credit: How it works and who [sic] it serves. https://www.urban.org/sites/default/files/publication/98758/lithc_how_it_works_and_who_it_serves_final_2.pdf

Schwartz, A. (2019). New York City's affordable housing plans and the limits of local initiative. *Cityscape, 21*(3), 355–388.

Schwartz, A. (2021). *Housing policy in the United States*. Routledge.

Servon, L. (2017). *The unbanking of America: How the new middle class survives*. Houghton Mifflin Harcourt.

Shanholtz, S. (2016). Do Qualified Allocation Plans influence developers' LIHTC siting decisions?: The case of access to high-performing schools. [Unpublished master's thesis]. Virginia Tech. Blacksburg, VA.

Shapiro, T. (2017). *Toxic inequality: How America's wealth gap destroys mobility, deepens the racial divide, and threatens our future*. Basic Books.

Shaw, R. (2018). *Generation priced out: Who gets to live in the new urban America*. University of California Press.

Sherman, R. (2017). *Uneasy street: The anxieties of affluence*. Princeton University Press.

Shibut, L. (2017). Resolution and receiverships. In F. Carns (Ed.), *Crisis and response: An FDIC history, 2008–2013* (pp. 175–239). Federal Deposit Insurance Corporation.

Shiller, R. J. (2008). *The subprime solution: How today's Global Financial Crisis happened, and what to do about it*. Princeton University Press.

Shmerling, R. H. (2022). *Why life expectancy in the US is falling: COVID-19 and drug overdoses are the biggest contributors*. https://www.health.harvard.edu/blog/why-life-expectancy-in-the-us-is-falling-202210202835#:~:text=With%20rare%20exceptions%2C%20life%20expectancy, year%20span%20since%20the%201920s.

Silver, H. (2012). Cooperative housing. In A. T. Carswell (Ed.), *The encyclopedia of housing* (pp. 101–107). SAGE.

Skeel, D. (2011). *The new financial deal: Understanding the Dodd-Frank Act and its (unintended) consequences*. John Wiley & Sons, Inc.

Snowden, K. A. (1997). Building and Loan Associations in the U.S., 1880–1893: The origins of localization in the residential mortgage market. *Research in Economics, 51*, 227–250.

Snowden, K. A. (2003). The transition from building and loan to saving and loan, 1890–1940. In S. L. Engerman, P. T. Hoffman, J.-L. Rosenthal, & K. L. Sokoloff (Eds.), *Finance, intermediaries, and economic development* (pp. 157–206). Cambridge University Press.

Speakman, M. (2018, November 6). *Uneven recovery: Many high-foreclosure ZIP codes haven't bounced back.* https://www.zillow.com/research/high-foreclo-sure-areas-recovering-21904/

Special Inspector General for the Troubled Asset Relief Program (2021). *Evaluation report: Treasury's public reporting on the Home Affordable Modification Program.* https://www.sigtarp.gov/sites/sigtarp/files/2021-08/SIGTARP-21-002_Treasury%27s%20Public%20Reporting%20on%20HAMP.pdf

Squires, G. (Ed).. (2018). *The fight for fair housing: Causes, consequences, and future implications of the 1968 Federal Fair Housing Act.* Routledge.

Stanton, T. H. (2012). Government-sponsored enterprises. In A. T. Carswell (Ed.), *The encyclopedia of housing* (pp. 245–249). SAGE.

Sternberg, J. C. (2019). *The theft of a decade: How the Baby Boomers stole the Millennials' economic future.* Public Affairs.

Stone, M. E. (2006). Housing affordability: One-third of a nation shelter poor. In R. G. Bratt, M. E. Stone, & C. Hartman (Eds.), *A right to housing: Foundation for a new social agenda* (pp. 38–60). Temple University Press.

Stone, M. E. (2009a). *Renter affordability in the city of Boston.* Center for Social Policy.

Stone, M. E. (2009b). Unaffordable "affordable housing": Challenging the U.S. Department of Housing and Urban Developments area median income. *Progressive Planning, 180*(Summer), 36–39.

Stout, D., Clogston, F., Thackeray, A., Stoloff, J., Anthony, B., & Hayes, C. (2019). *Final report: Evaluation of HUD's Rental Assistance Demonstration (RAD).* https://www.huduser.gov/portal/publications/RAD-Evaluation-Final-Report.html

Straus, E. E. (2014). *Death of a suburban dream: Race and schools in Compton, California.* University of Pennsylvania Press.

Stueve, C., Seay, M. C., & Carswell, A. T. (2018). Renting. In K. B. Anacker, A. T. Carswell, S. D. Kirby, & K. R. Tremblay (Eds.), *Introduction to housing* (pp. 156–166). University of Georgia Press.

Sullivan, E. (2018). *Manufactured insecurity: Mobile home parks and Americans' tenuous right to place.* University of California Press.

Swarns, R. L. (2008, April 30). Federal mortgage plan falls short, critics say. *New York Times.*

Talen, E. (2019). *Neighborhood.* Oxford University Press.

Tax Policy Center (2018). *Impact on itemized deductions of the Tax Cuts and Jobs Act*. https://www.taxpolicycenter.org/model-estimates/impact-itemized-deductions-tax-cuts-and-jobs-act-jan-2018/t18-0001-impact-number

Taylor, K.-Y. (2019). *Race for profit: How banks and the real estate industry undermined Black homeownership*. The University of North Carolina Press.

Taylor, P. (2014). *The next America: Boomers, Millennials, and the looming generational showdown*. Public Affairs.

Teck, A. (1968). *Mutual savings banks and savings and loan associations: Aspects of growth*. Columbia University Press.

The Living New Deal (n.d.). *Public Works Administration (PWA) (1933)*. https://livingnewdeal.org/glossary/public-works-administration-pwa-1933-1943/

Thompson, D. (2022, August 18). *Why the rent inflation is so damn high: It's just the latest chapter in the "everything is weird" economy*. https://www.theatlantic.com/ideas/archive/2022/08/rent-inflation-housing-demand-prices/671179/

Thomson, J. B., & Koepke, M. (2010, September 23). *Federal Home Loan Banks: The Housing GSEs that didn't bark in the night: Economic trends*. https://www.clevelandfed.org/en/newsroom-and-events/publications/economic-trends/economic-trends-archives/2010-economic-trends/et-20100923-federal-home-loan-banks-the-housing-gse-that-didnt-bark-in-the-night.aspx

Torres, L. (2019, July 14). Simple ways to prevent falls in older adults. National Public Radio.

Tracey, M. D. (2023, March 14). *How 3 recent bank failures could impact housing market*. https://www.nar.realtor/magazine/real-estate-news/how-3-recent-bank-failures-could-impact-housing-market

Turner, M. A., Santos, R., Levy, D. K., Wissoker, D., Aranda, C., & Pitingolo, R. (2013). *Housing discrimination against racial and ethnic minorities 2012*. https://www.huduser.gov/portal/Publications/pdf/HUD-514_HDS2012.pdf

Umbach, F., & Gerould, A. (2015). Myth #3: Public housing breeds crime. In N. D. Bloom, F. Umbach, & L. J. Vale (Eds.), *Public housing myths: Perception, reality, and social policy* (pp. 64–90). Cornell University Press.

UNHABITAT (n.d.). *The right to adequate housing: Fact sheet No. 21 (Revision 1)*. https://www.ohchr.org/Documents/Publications/FS21_rev_1_Housing_en.pdf

United Nations (n.d.). *Universal Declaration of Human Rights*. https://www.un.org/en/universal-declaration-human-rights/

United Nations Human Rights: Office of the High Commissioner (n.d.a). *Special Rapporteur on adequate housing as a component of the right to an adequate standard of living, and on the right to non-discrimination in this context*. https://www.ohchr.org/EN/Issues/Housing/Pages/HousingIndex.aspx

United Nations Human Rights: Office of the High Commissioner (n.d.b). *Current and former mandate-holders for existing mandates valid as of 1 May 2019.* https://www.ohchr.org/EN/HRBodies/SP/Pages/Currentmandateholders.aspx

United Nations Human Rights: Office of the High Commissioner (n.d.c). *Special Rapporteur on adequate housing as a component of the right to an adequate standard of living, and on the right of non-discrimination in this context: Ms. Farha.* https://www.ohchr.org/EN/Issues/Housing/Pages/HousingIndex.aspx

United Nations Human Rights: Office of the High Commissioner (n.d.d). *Annual reports: Adequate housing.* https://www.ohchr.org/en/issues/housing/pages/annualreports.aspx

Urban Institute (n.d.). *Housing Credit Availability Index.* https://www.urban.org/policy-centers/housing-finance-policy-center/projects/housing-credit-availability-index

U.S. Bureau of the Census (n.d.a). *Historical data: New residential construction.* https://www.census.gov/construction/nrc/historical_data/index.html

U.S. Bureau of the Census (n.d.b). *Decennial Census of Population and Housing.* https://www.census.gov/programs-surveys/decennial-census.html#:~:text=The%20U.S.%20census%20counts%20each, of%20Representatives%20among%20the%20states.

U.S. Bureau of the Census (n.d.c). *Historical Census of Housing tables: Homeownership.* https://www.census.gov/history/www/reference/publications/historic_housing_data.html

U.S. Bureau of the Census (n.d.d). *Historical households tables.* https://www.census.gov/data/tables/time-series/demo/families/households.html

U.S. Bureau of the Census (n.d.e). *Table A-2: Households by total money income, race, and Hispanic origin of householders: 1967 to 2020.* https://www.census.gov/data/tables/2021/demo/income-poverty/p60-273.html

U.S. Bureau of the Census (1975). *Historical statistics of the United States: Colonial times to 1970.* https://www.census.gov/library/publications/1975/compendia/hist_stats_colonial-1970.html

U.S. Bureau of the Census (2018, November 14). *U.S. Census Bureau releases 2018 families and living arrangements tables.* https://www.census.gov/newsroom/press-releases/2018/families.html

U.S. Bureau of the Census (2023, January 31). *Quarterly residential vacancies and homeownership, fourth quarter 2022.* https://www.census.gov/housing/hvs/files/currenthvspress.pdf

U.S. Department of Agriculture (n.d.a). *Mutual self-help housing technical assistance grants.* https://www.rd.usda.gov/programs-services/mutual-self-help-housing-technical-assistance-rants#:~:text=What%20does%20this%20program%20do, own%20homes%20in%20rural%20areas.

U.S. Department of Agriculture (n.d.b). *WIC: COVID-19 waivers by state.* https://www.fns.usda.gov/disaster/pandemic/covid-19/wic-waivers-flexibilities

U.S. Department of Housing and Urban Development (n.d.a). *Community Development Block Grant (CDBG) Program*. https://www.hud.gov/program_offices/comm_planning/communitydevelopment

U.S. Department of Housing and Urban Development (n.d.b). *HOME Investment Partnerships Program*. https://www.hud.gov/program_offices/comm_planning/affordablehousing/programs/home/

U.S. Department of Housing and Urban Development (n.d.c). *Community Development Block Grant Entitlement Program*. https://www.hudexchange.info/programs/cdbg-entitlement/

U.S. Department of Housing and Urban Development (n.d.d). *Housing Choice Vouchers fact sheet*. https://www.hud.gov/program_offices/public_indian_housing/programs/hcv/about/fact_sheet

U.S. Department of Housing and Urban Development (n.d.e). *"Lead Speak": A brief glossary*. https://files.hudexchange.info/resources/documents/MakingItWorkReferenceManual.pdf

U.S. Department of Housing and Urban Development (n.d.f). *Fair Market Rents*. https://www.huduser.gov/portal/datasets/fmr.html

U.S. Department of Housing and Urban Development (n.d.g). *The Federal Housing Administration (FHA)*. https://www.hud.gov/federal_housing_administration

U.S. Department of Housing and Urban Development (n.d.h). *Disease risks and homelessness*. https://www.hudexchange.info/homelessness-assistance/diseases/

U.S. Department of Housing and Urban Development (n.d.i). *NSP basics*. https://www.hudexchange.info/programs/nsp/nsp-eligibility-requirements/

U.S. Department of Housing and Urban Development (n.d.j). *U.S. Department of Housing and Urban Development 1930–2020*. https://www.huduser.gov/hud_timeline/

U.S. Department of Housing and Urban Development (n.d.k). *Choice Neighborhoods*. https://www.hud.gov/cn

U.S. Department of Housing and Urban Development (n.d.l). *Community planning and development appropriation budget/allocations*. https://www.hud.gov/program_offices/comm_planning/budget

U.S. Department of Housing and Urban Development (n.d.m). *RAD resident fact sheets*. https://www.hud.gov/RAD/residents/ResidentFactSheets#:~:text=The%20Rental%20Assistance%20Demonstration%20(RAD, is%20tied%20to%20the%20property.

U.S. Department of Housing and Urban Development (2008). *Mortgagee letter 2008–41*. https://www.hud.gov/sites/documents/DOC_23764.doc

U.S. Department of Housing and Urban Development (2010). *Fact sheet: Hope for Homeowners to provide additional mortgage assistance to struggling homeowners*. https://archives.hud.gov/initiatives/hopeforhomeowners/pressfactsheet.cfm

U.S. Department of Housing and Urban Development (2012). *FY 2012 agency financial report*. https://www.hud.gov/program_offices/cfo/afr_fy2012

U.S. Department of Housing and Urban Development (2016). *Federal Housing Administration annual report to Congress: The financial status of the FHA Mutual Mortgage Insurance Fund fiscal year 2016.* https://www.hud.gov/sites/documents/2016FHAANNUALREPORT1.PDF

U.S. Department of Housing and Urban Development (2017a, August 14). *Defining housing affordability.* https://www.huduser.gov/portal/pdredge/pdr-edge-featd-article-081417.html

U.S. Department of Housing and Urban Development (2017b, January 20). *Mortgagee letter 2017-07.* https://archives.hud.gov/news/2017/17-07ml.pdf

U.S. Department of Housing and Urban Development (2018, June 6). *Low-Income Housing Tax Credits.* https://www.huduser.gov/portal/datasets/lihtc.html

U.S. Department of Housing and Urban Development (2021). *Reminder guidance for FHA-approved mortgagees regarding Presidentially-Declared Major Disaster Areas.* https://www.hud.gov/sites/dfiles/SFH/documents/SFH_FHA_INFO_21-74.pdf

U.S. Department of Housing and Urban Development (2022). *Annual report to Congress regarding the financial status of the FHA Mutual Mortgage Insurance Fund: Fiscal Year 2022.* https://www.hud.gov/sites/dfiles/Housing/documents/2022FHAAnnualRptMMIFund.pdf

U.S. Department of Housing and Urban Development (2023a). *Choice Neighborhoods.* https://www.hud.gov/sites/dfiles/CFO/documents/2024_CJ_Program_Template_-_Choice_Neighborhoods.pdf

U.S. Department of Housing and Urban Development (2023b). *HOME Investment Partnerships Program.* https://www.hud.gov/sites/dfiles/CFO/documents/2023_CJ_Program_-_HOME_updated.pdf

U.S. Department of Housing and Urban Development (2023c). *FHA single family market share.* https://www.hud.gov/sites/dfiles/Housing/images/FHASFMarketShare2023Q1.pdf

U.S. Department of Labor (n.d.a). *Employee rights: Paid sick leave and expanded family and medical leave under the Families First Coronavirus Response Act.* https://www.dol.gov/sites/dolgov/files/WHD/posters/FFCRA_Poster_WH1422_Non-Federal.pdf

U.S. Department of Labor (n.d.b). *Federal employee rights: Paid sick leave and expanded family and medical leave under the Families First Coronavirus Response Act.* https://www.dol.gov/sites/dolgov/files/WHD/posters/FFCRA_Poster_WH1422_Federal.pdf

U.S. Department of Veterans Affairs (n.d.). *VA home loans.* https://www.benefits.va.gov/homeloans/

U.S. Environmental Protection Agency (n.d.a). *Protect your family from exposures to asbestos.* https://www.epa.gov/asbestos/protect-your-family-exposures-asbestos

U.S. Environmental Protection Agency (n.d.b). *Protect your family from exposures to lead.* https://www.epa.gov/lead/protect-your-family-exposures-lead

U.S. Environmental Protection Agency (n.d.c). *Learn about mold.* https://www.epa.gov/mold

U.S. Environmental Protection Agency (n.d.d). *A citizen's guide to radon: The guide to protecting yourself and your family from radon.* https://www.epa.gov/radon/citizens-guide-radon-guide-protecting-yourself-and-your-family-radon

U.S. Environmental Protection Agency (n.d.e). *EPA radon zones (with state information).* https://www.epa.gov/radon/epa-map-radon-zones

Vale, L. J. (2000). *From the puritans to the projects: Public housing and public neighbors.* Harvard University Press.

Vespa, J., Medina, L., & Armstrong, D. M. (2020). *Demographic turning points for the United States: Population projections for 2020 to 2060: Population estimates and projections: Current population reports.* https://www.census.gov/content/dam/Census/library/publications/2020/demo/p25-1144.pdf

Von Hoffman, A. (2003). *House by house, block by block: The rebirth of America's urban neighborhoods.* Oxford University Press.

Wallace, M. (2017). *Greater Gotham: A history of New York City from 1898 to 1919.* Oxford University Press.

Wallison, P. J. (2011). Eliminating the GSEs as part of comprehensive housing finance reform. In M. N. Baily (Ed.), *The future of housing finance: Restructuring the U.S. residential mortgage market* (pp. 92–110). Brookings Institution Press.

Wang, R., & Balachandran, S. (2023). Inclusionary housing in the United States: Dynamics of local policy and outcomes in diverse Markets. *Housing Studies, 38*(6), 1068–1087.

Warren, E. (2007). Unsafe at any rate: If it's good enough for microwaves, it's good enough for mortgages. Why we need a financial product safety commission. *Democracy, n.v.*, 5, 8–19.

Warren, E., & Tyagi, A. W. (2003). *The two-income trap: Why middle-class parents are going broke.* Basic Books.

Watkins, T. H. (1993). *The Great Depression: America in the 1930s.* Back Bay Books.

Weber, R. (2015). *From boom to bubble: How finance built the new Chicago.* The University of Chicago Press.

Wedeen, S. (2023, July 6). *Low-cost rentals have decreased in every state.* Blog. https://www.jchs.harvard.edu/blog/low-cost-rentals-have-decreased-every-state?fbclid=IwAR1B-lf6nf2qucksjdvUe0PS1Dz5nkjJJ2tcFzo8rGvXSTZNwHGfgM6HoM4

Wehrmann, J. (2022, October 24). *Fannie Mae and Freddie Mac will require the use of FICO® Score 10 T.* https://www.fico.com/blogs/fannie-mae-and-freddie-mac-will-require-use-fico-score-10-t

Weicher, J. C. (2012). *Housing policy at a crossroads: The why, how, and who of assistance programs.* The AEI Press.

Weinstein, A. (2019, September 6). Fannie-Freddie investors fighting profit sweep get key win. https://www.bloomberg.com/news/articles/2019-09-06/fannie-freddie-investors-get-key-win-in-bid-to-end-profit-sweep

Weinstock, L. R. (2023, January 3). *Introduction to U.S. economy: Housing market.* https://sgp.fas.org/crs/misc/IF11327.pdf

Weiss, M. A. (2002). *The rise of the community builders: The American real estate industry and urban land planning.* Beard Books.

Whelan, C. K. (2018). The end of the Home Affordable Modification Program and the start of a new problem. *Brooklyn Law Review, 83*(4), 1469–1496.

Wherry, F. F., Seefeldt, K. S., & Alvarez, A. S. (2019). *Credit where it's due: Rethinking financial citizenship.* Russell Sage Foundation.

Whittemore, A. H., & Curran-Groome, W. (2022). Review essay: A case of (decreasing) American Exceptionalism: Single-family zoning in the United States, Australia, and Canada. *Journal of the American Planning Association, 88*(3), 335–351.

Wiese, A. (2004). *Places of their own: African American suburbanization in the twentieth century.* The University of Chicago Press.

Wilkerson, I. (2010). *The warmth of other suns: The epic story of America's great migration.* Vintage Books.

Wilkerson, I. (2020). *Caste: The origins of our discontents.* Random House.

Williamson, A. R. (2011). Can they afford the rent? Resident cost burden in Low Income Housing Tax Credit developments. *Urban Affairs Review, 47*(6), 775–799.

Willse, C. (2015). *The value of homelessness: Managing surplus life in the United States.* University of Minnesota Press.

World Health Organization (n.d.). *Global Health Observatory (GHO): Female life expectancy.* https://apps.who.int/gho/data/node.main.688

Wright, C. D. (1894). *Ninth annual report of the Commissioner of Labor: Building and loan associations.* Government Printing Office.

Xiong, S. (2017). Key housing issues facing immigrant communities in the Twin Cities: Interviews with leaders from the Hmong, Latino and Somali Communities. https://www.mhponline.org/images/Immigrant-research-final.pdf

Xu, J., Murphy, S. L., Kochanek, K. D., & Arias, E. (2022). *Mortality in the United States, 2021.* https://www.cdc.gov/nchs/products/databriefs/db456.htm

Zandi, M. (2009). *Financial shock: Global panic and government bailouts: How we got here and what must be done to fix it.* FT Press.

Zillow (2012, May 24). *Despite home value gains, underwater homeowners owe $1.2 trillion more than homes' worth.* http://zillow.mediaroom.com/2012-05-24-Despite-Home-Value-Gains-Underwater-Homeowners-Owe-1-2-Trillion-More-than-Homes-Worth

INDEX

Note: *Italic* page numbers refer to figures.

For Product Safety Concerns and Information please contact our EU representative GPSR@taylorandfrancis.com Taylor & Francis Verlag GmbH, Kaufingerstraße 24, 80331 München, Germany

Printed and bound by CPI Group (UK) Ltd, Croydon, CR0 4YY

08/06/2025

01897000-0007